MY FATHER'S NAMES

MY FATHER'S NAMES

The Old Testament Names of God and How They Can Help You Know Him More Intimately

ELMER L. TOWNS

Regal

A Division of Gospel Light
Ventura, California, U.S.A.

Published by Regal Books
A Division of Gospel Light
Ventura, California 93006
Printed in U.S.A.

Unless otherwise indicated, Scripture quotations in this book are taken from
the *King James Version*, public domain.

Other versions used are:
NKJV—New King James Version, Holy Bible, Copyright © 1979, 1980, 1982 by
Thomas Nelson Inc., Publishers. Used by permission.
NIV—Scripture quotations marked (NIV) are from the HOLY BIBLE, NEW INTER-
NATIONAL VERSION. Copyright © 1973, 1978, 1984 International Bible Society.
Used by permission of Zondervan Bible Publishers.

Library of Congress Cataloging-in-Publication Data

Towns, Elmer L.,
    My Father's Names / Elmer L. Towns.
      p.   cm.
    ISBN 0-8307-1447-2
    1. God—Name—Biblical teaching. 2. Bible. O.T.—Criticism, inter-
    pretation, etc.   I. Title.
    BS1192.6.T69   1991
    231'.014—dc20   91-2834
                                                  CIP

11 12 13 14 15 / 01 00 99 98 97 96

Rights for publishing this book in other languages are contracted by Gospel Lit-
erature International (GLINT). GLINT also provides technical help for the adap-
tation, translation and publishing of Bible study resources and books in scores of
languages worldwide. For further information, contact GLINT, P.O. Box 4060,
Ontario, CA 91761-1003, U.S.A., or the publisher.

❧ CONTENTS ❧

❖ INTRODUCTION ❖

Can you imagine two persons really getting to know and love each other without knowing each other's names? Somehow, our name becomes so intertwined with our personality that only those who know our name can truly love and understand us.

This is no less true in our relationship with God. Yet many of us have not taken the time to get to know and love God by becoming familiar with the many names by which He is known in Scripture. This book is therefore a guide for those who want to come to know Him more intimately.

There are three primary names of God in the Old Testament: God (*Elohim*), Lord (*Jehovah*, or *Yahweh*) and Lord/Master (*Adonai*). Beyond these, God is called by over 80 other compound names or descriptive titles. The names are studied here as they first appear in Scripture.

In chapter 1 the primary names are examined, and this becomes a foundation for the rest of the book. Next, eight important names of God are surveyed through the structure of Psalm 23, under the general title "The Lord Is My Shepherd." Then other names of God are surveyed, one name in each chapter (chaps. 3—8), corresponding roughly to the time when the name was introduced to God's people in the Old Testament.

The final chapters are climactic, studying the primary names of God in depth, building on what has gone before. Chapter 9 examines our slave relationship to Adonai, the Lord/Master. Chapter 10 looks at the name Elohim and answers the question, Who is God? by defining His nature. Chapter 11 answers the question, What is God like? by examining the name Jehovah and describing His attributes. The last chapter is the capstone. It looks at the name Father, the New Testament name for God. All the Old Testament meanings of the names of God are wrapped up in the New Testament name, Father.

Although not every name of God is discussed in these 12 chapters, there is a short encyclopedic entry on each Old Testament name in Appendix A. The names of God chosen for study are those most discussed in the history of the Church and those that give the most significant insights into the person and nature of God.

This book was originally a series of Sunday School lessons that I taught in the Pastor's Bible Class at Thomas Road Baptist Church in Lynchburg, Virginia. Senior Pastor Jerry Falwell says this is the largest Sunday School in America because of the thousands who attend in person and the almost 1 million who view it on television. Class members were caught up in the content of this series because it had so much material that was new to them. Theirs was not an infatuation with secret knowledge, but a yearning to know and approach God in prayer. Their response encouraged me to put the lessons in print so others could have this information and teach it in their classes. May this book help you understand God better and, as a result, may you become more dedicated to Him.

ELMER L. TOWNS
Lynchburg, Virginia

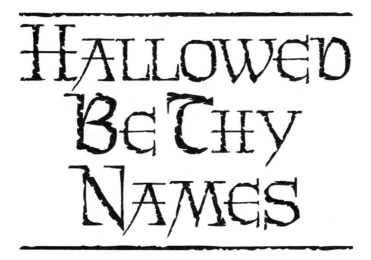

CHAPTER 1

HALLOWED BE THY NAMES

ONE evening I visited Mount Rushmore National Monument in South Dakota—and almost missed it. I had spoken at an evening meeting for pastors some 30 miles away, and after my message I asked one of the ministers to drive me to the monument. I did not know that the floodlights that illuminate the gigantic sculptures of Washington, Jefferson, Lincoln and Roosevelt were turned off at 11 o'clock. We arrived at the base of Mount Rushmore at 11:10 P.M.—10 minutes late. The spectacular carvings were veiled in darkness. As a result of an imminent storm, there wasn't even any moonlight.

But what I thought was a barrier became a blessing. Flashes of lightning accompanied the thunderstorm, and with each flash I got a quick glance at the great sculptures. I had certain preconceived images in mind from photographs, and I strained to compare each statue with the likeness in my mind's eye. The more I watched, the more I realized that I was appreciating their magnificence and grandeur even more than I would have if the storm had not forced me to view them more intensely.

In the same way, we struggle to understand God. We know He is there, but in the darkness of this life, we cannot see Him. Then come flashes of light that reveal Him—the creation...the miracles...the Ten Commandments...His presence in our conscience.

But there is another flash of illumination that is often overlooked. We can come to know God through His names. The many descriptive titles and names given in Scripture are like lightning flashes in a summer night, revealing His nature and works. We can get to know God better through His names.

Why does God have many names? Just as white light is made up of seven different rays or colors, so God is made up of different attributes that are illuminated by different names. Just as a person can examine each of the seven dif-

---

> *The many descriptive titles and names of God given in Scripture are like lightning flashes in a summer night, revealing His nature and works.*

---

ferent colors to understand the nature of light, so we need to examine each of God's attributes in order to better understand Him. Put together, the seven hues of light become white light, with the individual colors obscured to the unaided eye. The unity of light is its diversity, and only thus do we understand it. In much the same way, God's names combine to reveal the One God, divine in all His attributes.

WHY STUDY THE NAMES OF GOD?

We come to understand people by their names and titles. David, the man after God's heart, is better understood by a study of his various names or titles. Knowing that David is described as a shepherd, warrior, king, poet and musician helps us understand his character and gives us insight into David the man. He was the son of Jesse and a great grandson of Boaz. David was from the line of Judah, the royal line from which many of Israel's kings came and from which Jesus Christ was born.

In a similar way, studying God's names reveals His character to us more intimately. Among other names, for example, we know Him as Creator, Judge, Savior and Sustainer. By reflecting on His names, we can gain insight into His nature and understand more about how He works in our lives. While mortals cannot fathom His nature completely, God has revealed Himself through His Scriptures and has given us the Holy Spirit as a guide in knowing Him. While we remain human, we can only "know in part" (1 Cor. 13:12), and our limited understanding will never fully grasp all that an unlimited God is and does. But as we come to understand God's names, we approach closer in our understanding of God Himself.

A second reason for studying the names of God is in order to understand the different relationships we can have with Him. A young man calls his girlfriend "sweetheart," but after they marry they have a new relationship signified by a new name: "wife." She may have been Mary Jones, but after the marriage ceremony, if she follows the usual custom, she has a new name—perhaps Mary Livingston. Her new name tells everyone that she has a new relationship with her husband.

The names of God become meaningful as we adjust to new or growing relationships with Him. Usually God revealed a new name to people at a fork in their road of life. He would help people through a difficulty by allowing them to experience Him in a different way, through a new name.

Abraham seems to have learned more of the different

names of God than any other person in Scripture. Why? Because Abraham was pioneering new trails in the walk of faith. Each time God wanted Abraham to reach higher, He revealed a new name. Abraham had known Him as the LORD (*Jehovah*, or *Yahweh*—Gen. 13:4); but when he tithed to Melchizedek, Abraham learned a new name: *El Elyon*, the Most High God, possessor of heaven and earth (14:18,19).

When Abraham complained to God in prayer that he did not have an heir for the promised inheritance, God revealed another of His names—*Adonai*, Master or Lord (15:2). The eternal LORD God of heaven would care for Abraham in a Master-slave relationship. Later, Abraham learned that God would nurture and powerfully sustain him as *El Shaddai* (17:1); that the secret name of God is *El Olam* (21:33); and that God would provide for him as *Jehovah-jireh* (22:14). Each time Abraham entered into a deeper relationship with God, he learned a new attribute of God through a new divine name.

A third reason for studying the names of God is that through His names God reveals that He is the source and solution to our problems. When Israel fought Amalek, they learned the name *Jehovah Nissi*, the LORD Our Banner, meaning that God would and could protect them (Exod. 17:15). As each name of God is unfolded, a new source of strength is revealed to His people. Moses learned the name *Jehovah Rophe* (from *rapha*, to heal), meaning that God would provide healing for the people (15:26). Later, Gideon learned of God as *Jehovah Shalom*, revealing a God of peace to a young man who was fearful and unsure of himself (Judg. 6:24).

Finally, the various names of God teach us to look to Him in our crises. God revealed His different names in times of crisis to reveal how He would help His servants.

Christians sometimes seem to think that they are immune to problems—that salvation solves them all. Of course this is shown to be untrue when problems or crises arise and we find ourselves crying out, Why me? Why now? Why this?

God allows people to have problems for a number of reasons. Sometimes He wants to test us, to see if we will handle problems by faith or in our own strength. At other times He allows problems to overwhelm us so we will turn to Him. In our crises, God reveals Himself anew, just as He originally revealed Himself through His names when His people needed help. If we know God's names, we can more freely turn to Him in the name that fits our situation.

THE THREE PRIMARY NAMES OF GOD

The following chart shows some facts about the three primary names or titles of God revealed in the Old Testament.

The Primary Names of God

Hebrew	English	First Reference	Root	Meaning
Elohim	God	Genesis 1:1	alah–to swear, or bind with an oath	Strong Creator
Jehovah	LORD	Genesis 2:4	hayah–to become, or to continue to reveal oneself	Self-existent One who reveals Himself
Adonai	Lord	Genesis 15:2	to be a master	The master of a slave

Beyond these primary names, many compound names also refer to God. As we have noted, God has different names to show us different aspects of His nature, or different ways He relates to us. Names and titles function this way among us, as well. Ruth Forbes became my wife, and her name became Ruth Towns. The new name reflected new duties, and a new and intimate relationship to me. We became one flesh. Then Ruth Towns became a mother. My new baby daughter called her, "Mother," a different name with new responsibilities and new intimacies.

The people of God first began using *Elohim* as a primary name for God the Creator. As they walked with God, they learned that He was also LORD, or Jehovah, the Self-existent One. Later they learned that He was Adonai, their Master. (Some scholars believe that Jehovah or Yahweh [the LORD] is actually the only proper, personal name for God, and that all other names are just descriptive titles.) A brief overview of all three names will introduce all that will follow in this book.

Elohim, the All-powerful Creator

The first reference to God in Scripture uses the name Elohim: "In the beginning God [Elohim] created..." (Gen. 1:1). This name for God is a reference to the supreme Being, the original Creator, the perfect Being, the eternal One. Just as most religions describe their divinities in terms of ultimate power (i.e., God), Elohim focuses on several aspects of power, strength or creativity. The Hebrew word Elohim is from *El*, the strong One or the Creator, or *alah*, to swear or bind oneself with an oath (implying faithfulness). Therefore when we call the Creator, God, we are referring to His strength or omnipotence. He is all powerful, more powerful than any person in the universe. Nothing is equal to Him in power.

Elohim appears 31 times in the first chapter of Genesis, because there His creative power is emphasized. "God saw" (1:4), "God called" (v. 5), "God said" (v. 6), "God made" (v. 7), "God blessed" (v. 22) and "God created man in his own image" (v. 27).

The names of God in the Bible indicate that He has personality, that He is a Being with intellect, emotion and will. To many people, God is not personal. Plato thought that God is eternal mind, the cause of all good in nature. Aristotle considered God the ground of all being. The German philosopher Hegel said that God is an impersonal being, just as a picture on the wall or a plate on the table. Spinoza, a pantheist, called God "the absolute universal substance," which means that He is the same thing as matter. Others have said that God is influence, power or energy. Some say that God is just an idea, with no real existence. But by revealing the names of God, the Old Testament presents Him as a powerful Person who thinks, feels and makes decisions; He has the attributes of personality.

Jehovah, the Self-existent One

The term LORD (spelled with a capital and small capitals in many translations) indicates the name Jehovah (or Yahweh), meaning "the Self-existent One." The root word is *hayah*, "to become." In Exodus 3:14 this root appears twice, as God identifies Himself as "I AM THAT I AM." Thus, God signifies that He alone is that Being who is self-existing—His existence depends on no other. The word hayah also implies that God is that Being who is continuously revealing Himself.

The name LORD or Jehovah is the most frequently used term for God in the Old Testament, appearing 6,823 times. The name I AM is always appropriate for God, since He has always existed in the past and will always exist in the future.

The Lord, Our Master

The third primary name for God is Lord (with only the first letter capitalized, to distinguish it from LORD), which is translated from the Hebrew word Adonai. This word comes from *adon*, which refers to the master of a slave. Hence Adonai indicates headship. When a person truly believes in God, that person also becomes a slave in service to his Lord, who has done so much for him. This title for God implies a twofold relationship: the Master can expect implicit obedience from the slave, and the slave can expect the Master to give him orders and to provide for his needs.

Jesus said, "Ye call me Master and Lord: and ye say well; for so I am" (John 13:13). Thus the believer is the slave of Christ, who has redeemed him. Since service is the issue in the master-slave relationship, the name Adonai is used in Scripture to indicate that believers are to minister for God.

COMPOUND NAMES FOR GOD

These three primary names of God are often joined together, or compounded, to communicate further insight into the person of God and how He cares for His people. Three of these are illustrated by the following expansion of the previously displayed chart.

Primary Names		
Elohim	God	Genesis 1:1
Jehovah	LORD	Genesis 2:4
Adonai	Lord/Master	Genesis 15:2

Compound Names		
LORD God	Jehovah Elohim	Genesis 2:4
Lord GOD	Adonai Jehovah	Genesis 15:2
Lord God	Adonai Elohim	Daniel 9:3

The name LORD God (Jehovah Elohim), which blends two major names for the Deity, is used distinctively in Scripture to indicate: (a) the relationship of God to man in Creation (see Gen. 2:7-15); (b) the moral authority of God over man (see vv. 16,17); (c) the One who controls man's earthly relationships (see vv. 18-24); and (d) the One who redeems man (see 3:8-15, 21).

The name Lord GOD (Adonai Jehovah) emphasizes the Adonai or Lordship characteristics of God, rather than His Jehovah traits. While He is still Creator, of course, the expression "the Lord GOD" indicates that He is Master of His people, as well.

The third compound name, Lord God (Adonai Elohim), refers to God as Master and Creator. This name means that God is the Master over all the false gods of other religions. When Daniel prays, "I set my face unto the Lord God" (Dan. 9:3), he is affirming that his Master (Adonai) is the God (Elohim) of false deities who claim to be God.

HOW THE JEWS USED GOD'S NAME

A study of the Hebrew proper names of God is more than a study of His titles. It is also a history of Israel's view of God. Since a people's view of God is a commentary on their view of their own life and culture, a study of the emerging Jewish use of the names for God is really a study of the Jews.

The various names of God represent a theology of God from the perspective of the Hebrew mind. According to the various Jewish encyclopedias, of all the names of God recorded in the Old Testament, the name Jehovah (or Yahweh) is God's distinctive personal name. The other names for God are actually titles, descriptions or reflections of His attributes.

In Old Testament times, the Jews felt that the divine name was equivalent to God's divine presence or power. The name of the LORD (Jehovah) was specially connected with the altar or the holy of holies, because that was the localized presence of God on earth. Instead of looking to

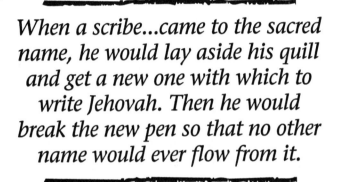

When a scribe...came to the sacred name, he would lay aside his quill and get a new one with which to write Jehovah. Then he would break the new pen so that no other name would ever flow from it.

pagan altars, the Israelites were to look to "the place which the LORD your God shall choose out of all your tribes to put his name there, even unto his habitation" (Deut. 12:5). Subdued enemies of God would eventually be brought to "the place of the name of the LORD of hosts, the mount Zion" (Isa. 18:7). So precious was the name of Jehovah that the people were not even to take the names of false gods upon their lips, lest they blaspheme the name of Jehovah by allowing both names to come out of the same mouth (see Exod. 23:13; Josh. 23:7).

According to early Jewish custom, the name of Jehovah was used in personal greetings, as "The LORD be with you," and "The LORD bless thee" (Ruth 2:4). But with time, the idolatry around them became a temptation. To reinforce their belief in monotheism, the rabbis came to recognize Jehovah as the only proper name for God, rather than Elohim or Adonai, which were considered only descriptive appellations of divinity.

Eventually the name Jehovah was considered too holy to pronounce, and the rabbis simply referred to it as "the Name." Others called it the "extraordinary name," the "distinguished name" or the "quadrilateral name" (or Tetragrammaton), for the four letters, YHWH. With the passing of time, the name Jehovah was pronounced only by the priests in the Temple when blessing the people (see Num. 6:23-27). Outside the Temple, they used the word Adonai.

The high priest also mentioned the name Jehovah on Yom Kippur, the Day of Atonement, 10 times, so that its pronunciation would not be lost. Also, older teachers repeated this name to their disciples once during every sabbatical year. They would have said, "This *is* my name for ever, and this *is* my memorial unto all generations" (Exod. 3:15). In teaching young theological students, the rabbis would write "for ever" (*olam*) defectively, rendering it *alam*, "to conceal," thus teaching their students that the name of God was to be concealed.

During the Maccabean uprising in the second century B.C., the Temple in Jerusalem was destroyed, and the priests ceased to pronounce the name altogether. Also because of the Maccabean revolt, occupying forces prohibited the utterance of "the Name." Later, when the Jews won relative independence, the rabbis decreed that the name could be used in certain formal notes and documents. Thus, Jehovah was identified regularly in everyday life. This practice, however, was soon discontinued because the rabbis thought that the name would be defiled when their notes were cancelled or thrown away—especially if they were found by someone who would profane or blaspheme the name. Consequently, the pronunciation of the name YHWH passed off the scene.

According to tradition, when the Jews wanted to distinguish Israelites from Samaritans, and later from Christians, they taught that the faithful would not pronounce the name. Slowly the doctrine arose that those who pronounced it were excluded from a share of the world to come. One rabbi said that whosoever explicitly pronounces the name is guilty of a capital offense.

Since the name of God was synonymous with holiness, to profane the name was a heinous sin. Another rabbi said that he who is guilty of profaning the name cannot rely on repentance, nor upon the power of the Day of Atonement to gain him expiation, nor upon sufferings to wipe it out; death alone can wipe it out. Yet another rabbi was even stricter, saying that the profaner of the name is classed among the five types of sinners for whom there is no forgiveness.

All kinds of practices grew up about writing the name Jehovah. When a scribe copying the Scriptures came to the sacred name, he would lay aside his quill and get a new one with which to write Jehovah. Then he would break the new pen so that no other name would ever flow from it, ensuring that the scribe could not be charged with blaspheming the name.

When Jesus came, He taught the multitudes to call on the name of the LORD God by addressing their prayers to the first Person of the Trinity. He taught people to use the intimate introduction in prayer, as in "Our Father which art in heaven, Hallowed be thy name" (Luke 11:1-4; emphasis on v. 2).

HALLOWING THE NAME TODAY

Several practical Christian applications flow from knowing the name of the LORD.

Prohibition Against Cursing

The Ten Commandments prohibit a person from taking God's name in vain. When a person lightly uses the name of God, he is speaking lightly of God. When a person blasphemes God's name, he blasphemes God. When a person curses by using God's name, he is either trying to take the place or authority of God or he is rejecting God's authority in his life. Because God's name represents His person, He said, "Thou shalt not take the name of the LORD thy God in vain" (Exod. 20:7).

Seeking God by His Name

The Bible clearly commands for us to "Be still, and know that I *am* God" (Ps. 46:10). Knowing God's name is a good way to know God, for it reveals to us the nature of His person and His work. As we are searching to know God, however, we should remember that He is also searching us and examining us. As David gave his son Solomon the plans for the Temple, he said, "Know thou the God of thy father, and serve him with a perfect heart...for the LORD searcheth all hearts, and understandeth all the imaginations of the thoughts: if thou seek him, he will be found of thee; but if thou forsake him, he will cast thee off for ever" (1 Chron. 28:9).

A person comes to God through Jesus Christ His Son, but even then God's name becomes important, for "as many as received him, to them gave he power to become the sons of God, *even* to them that believe on his name" (John 1:12). Later in the same Gospel, John says that he writes "that ye might believe,...and that believing ye might have life through His name" (20:31).

Gaining Knowledge of Ourselves

The Bible teaches that we are created in the image of God: "God created man in his *own* image, in the image of God created he him; male and female created he them" (Gen. 1:27). The more we learn about God, therefore, the more we learn about ourselves. Because we are created in God's image, we have a subconscious idea of God. But instead of recognizing God as our Master and submitting to Him, we strive subconsciously to take His place. That was the sin of Lucifer in wanting to be like the Most High (see Isa. 14:13,14). Since we have God's nature, the more we learn about Him the more we learn about ourselves.

Knowing God and Eternal Life

When Jesus prayed in the garden the night before His death, He said, "And this is life eternal, that they might know thee the only true God, and Jesus Christ, whom thou has sent" (John 17:3). It is impossible to know God without being saved. "Neither is there salvation in any other: for there is none other name under heaven given among men, whereby we must be saved" (Acts 4:12).

CHAPTER 2

◆ THE LORD IS MY SHEPHERD ◆

The Caring Name of God

WHEN the Bible says, "All we like sheep have gone astray" (Isa. 53:6), it compares us to dumb animals. You never see sheep in a circus because, as the animal trainer will tell you, it is almost impossible to train them to do tricks. They were not given protection like the quills of a porcupine, the scent of a skunk, the claws of a cat or the teeth of a lion. Of all the animals, sheep are characteristically the least protected. In water, their wool gets so soaked and heavy that it pulls them under and they easily drown. They have little instinct of danger and are susceptible to poisonous snake bites and infectious insect bites. They only lie down when they are full, and then if someone doesn't turn them over they may suffocate.

The total dependence of sheep upon the shepherd is why they are used as an illustration for the relationship between the Lord and believers. When Psalm 23:1 says "The Lord *is* my shepherd" it is speaking of *Jehovah Roi*, the faithful God who watches over us and cares for us. Notice that it is "the Lord" (Jehovah) who is our shepherd, not God. The use of the personal name Jehovah keys on God's intimacy with His people. Jehovah signifies the covenant-keeping God, and Roi refers to the way He tenderly cares for us.

Some have supposed that the Old Testament portrays God only in His awesome majesty, not as a God with the love and concern of a Father, as in the New Testament. But the picture of Jehovah Roi in Psalm 23 is of God as an intimate Father who cares for His own.

The two words Jehovah Roi are not a phrase consisting of the LORD's name attached to a noun or an adjective, indicating an actual title for God. The two words comprise a sentence indicating a function of God, or a description of what He does: "The LORD *is* my shepherd" (Ps. 23:1). As a matter of fact, Psalm 23 has several other descriptions that show God's care for His people. Each trait also appears elsewhere in Scripture, with a descriptive phrase or implied title for Jehovah, as the following chart shows.

Traits of God in Psalm 23

Function in Psalm 23	Implied Name or Trait	Reference
The LORD *is* my shepherd (v. 1)	*Jehovah Roi*	Psalm 23:1
I shall not want (v. 2)	*Jehovah-jireh* (The LORD Shall Provide)	Genesis 22:14
He leadeth me beside the still waters (v. 2)	*Jehovah Shalom* (The LORD [Our] Peace)	Judges 6:24
He restoreth my soul (v. 3)	*Jehovah Rophe* (The LORD [Our] Healer)	Exodus 15:26
He leadeth me in the paths of righteousness (v. 3)	*Jehovah Tsidkenu* (The LORD Our Righteousness)	Jeremiah 23:6
I will fear no evil (v. 4)	*Jehovah Nissi* (The LORD My Banner)	Exodus 17:15
Thou *art* with me (v. 4)	*Jehovah Shammah* (The LORD Is There)	Ezekiel 48:35
Thou anointest my head with oil (v. 5)	*Jehovah Mekaddishkhem* (The LORD that Sanctifies You)	Exodus 31:13

Notice that each divine function corresponds to a deep human need. Psalm 23 is structured to show that our needs are matched by the caring response of God. Taking each of the above human needs and its corresponding divine trait in order, let us see what they tell us of the caring God of Psalm 23, and how He meets our needs.

THE GOD WHO MEETS OUR NEEDS

Protection: *Jehovah Roi*

The Bible's first reference to God as a Shepherd is in a statement made by Jacob in Genesis 48:15, when he speaks of "the God which fed [shepherded] me all my life long." Even though Jacob had wandered far from God, as a sheep wanders from the pasture or the shepherd, God had been Jacob's shepherd all along. As an older man, Jacob realized that he had experienced Jehovah Roi.

What are sheep like? When Isaiah said that "All we like sheep have gone astray; we have turned every one to his own way" (53:6), he referred first to the fact that they are directionless, with no sense of where home is. Second, sheep have little sense of danger and are generally ignorant in matters of self-preservation. A sheep will wander too close to the den of a wolf, or get caught in a thicket of briars, or wander out into swift water where its fluffy fleece will first float it away, then weigh it down to be drowned. Because we, like sheep, do not know how to protect ourselves, we need Jehovah Roi, the divine Shepherd.

This threefold nature of sheep means that a shepherd has a threefold task. Under the leadership of Jehovah Roi, the Good Shepherd, earthly shepherds or pastors also help fulfill this function. First, they lead the sheep by example. The power of a godly role model is great. Good pastors lead the flock "beside the still waters" (Ps. 23:2), so the sheep can "drink" of Jesus Christ, have fellowship with Him and build up their spirituality. Shepherds also lead the sheep "in the paths of righteousness for his name's sake" (v. 3). This is leadership away from sin and toward true godliness.

Second, a shepherd feeds his sheep by guiding them into green pastures or by picking clover and feeding them by hand. Earthly pastors feed the flock by teaching and explaining the Word to the people. Jesus reminded Peter of his responsibility in this area three times (see John 21:15-

---

Believers who are tormented by their feelings need to know Jehovah Shalom, the LORD [Our] Peace.

---

17). He was to be an example to the flock, to teach and preach the Word of God and to tend the sheep.

Third, the shepherd tends his flock by protecting the sheep. Earthly shepherds protect the sheep by rebuke, warning and counsel, helping them guard against sin.

Bread: *Jehovah-jireh*
"I shall not want" (Ps. 23:1). Life's basic needs are provided by Jehovah-jireh, "The LORD Shall Provide."

When Jesus taught His disciples to pray, "Give us this day our daily bread" (Matt. 6:11), He was including all of our daily needs. "Bread" meant food, water, clothing, a roof over our heads, strength for the journey and anything else needed to keep body and soul together. These provisions are from Jehovah-jireh.

God also provides what we need to offer Him in the

way of sacrifice. In this context we can note that the phrase Jehovah-jireh is one of the few names for God that is given by man, rather than revealed by God Himself. Abraham had been commanded to take his son Isaac to Mount Moriah and to sacrifice him to the LORD (see Gen. 22). In obedience, and as an act of faith, Abraham took his son to the point of death, even lifting the knife for the ultimate sacrifice. But Jehovah-jireh stopped him and provided "a ram caught in a thicket by his horns" (v. 13). Abraham took the ram and offered it to God. Then "Abraham called the name of the place, The-LORD-Will-Provide [Jehovah-jireh]; as it is said *to* this day, 'In the Mount of The LORD it shall be provided'" (v. 14, *NKJV*).

When young Isaac had asked about the lamb for the sacrifice, his father Abraham had promised, "My son, God will provide himself a lamb for a burnt-offering" (v. 8). Some translators place the comma differently and translate this verse, "God will provide himself, [as] a lamb for a burnt-offering." Although the Hebrew literally says "God will provide *for Himself* the lamb for a burnt-offering," the fact is true that God did give Himself through His Son Jesus Christ as the offering for the sins of the world (see Zech. 12:10; John 1:29; 3:16). In this sense, Jesus Christ was the ultimate provision of Jehovah-jireh, the God who supplies both our physical and our spiritual needs.

Emotional Upsets: *Jehovah Shalom*

"He leadeth me beside still waters" (Ps. 23:2). This is a function of Jehovah Shalom, "The LORD [Our] Peace." The LORD takes care of us in times of discouragement and in the emotional storms of life. Believers who are tormented by their feelings need to know Jehovah Shalom, The LORD [Our] Peace. In the midst of difficult and pressure-filled situations, "He maketh [us] to lie down" (v. 2) inside, in our hearts, resting in His solution.

The phrase Jehovah Shalom was revealed when Gideon faced a task that was too great for him. The Lord came to Gideon and told him that he was to lead his people in victory over the Midianites. Gideon felt he was too small for the task. He complained that he was the youngest son in his father's family, and that theirs was the least family in the tribe of Manasseh, which was the least of the 12 tribes of Israel. But God revealed Himself to Gideon, which is always enough to get the task done. Because of that revelation Gideon said, "Alas, O Lord God! For I have seen the Angel of the Lord face to face" (Judg. 6:22, *NKJV*).

God responded to Gideon, "Peace *be* with you; do not fear, you shall not die" (v. 23, *NKJV*). Then Gideon built an altar there to the Lord, and called it "The-Lord-Shalom" (v. 24, *NKJV*), which means Jehovah [Is Our] Peace. Again, a man gave a new name to Jehovah to explain His help in the face of a crisis. Gideon learned that when he faced a task that was fearful or threatening, Jehovah Shalom could bring peace to his heart.

When Gideon built an altar before gathering an army or forming a battle plan, he was exercising faith. The only way a person can have the peace of Jehovah Shalom is by faith. "Therefore being justified by faith, we have peace with God through our Lord Jesus Christ" (Rom. 5:1). Then as we attempt to live for God after we are saved, the Bible says, "the God of peace shall be with you" (Phil. 4:9; compare "Jehovah Shalom").

A shepherd once observed that sheep only lie down when they are full. And, as we have noted, they cannot be left lying down by themselves too long, lest they roll over and suffocate in their own wool or be attacked and infected by poisonous insects or snakes. Jehovah Shalom enables the sheep to lie down in safety. And since they are afraid of swiftly running water, He makes them lie down by still water.

Healing: *Jehovah Rophe*

"He restoreth my soul" (Ps. 23:3). The LORD who is a shepherd heals His sick sheep, restoring them to wholeness. In this work He is Jehovah Rophe, "The LORD [Our] Healer." Whereas some animals have self-protective instincts, sheep have little or none. Most are not aware of the fact that they have been hurt, or that they are sick. It takes a shepherd to know that they need healing, and to care for them.

The phrase Jehovah Rophe, "The LORD [Our] Healer" ("The LORD that healeth thee") occurs in Exodus 15:26. Moses, God's shepherd for Israel, led the multitude through the Red Sea into the wilderness. For three days the people found no water. This can be a terrifying and life-threatening experience. Finally the people came to a pool of water called Marah, but its waters were bitter and they complained.

Bitter water can mean water that is not acceptable to the taste, but is not harmful. Or it can mean water that is contaminated and dangerous. Apparently both are implied here. Upon God's instructions, Moses found a tree, cut it down and threw it into the water. God often works through symbols in this way, using that which is visible to accomplish His inner workings. The tree could have had an agent that actually sweetened the water, or it could have been a visible symbol of the miracle of God that made the waters fit to drink. In either case, He used the incident to teach a lesson: the LORD can heal.

From this healing of the waters, Jehovah Rophe teaches of His power over illness. First, He "heals" through preventative medicine. "I will put none of these diseases upon thee," He promises (v. 26), meaning that if the Israelites follow Him, He will keep them from the plagues inflicted upon the Egyptians. The condition was, "If thou wilt diligently hearken to the voice of the LORD thy God" (v. 26).

Many Christians have enjoyed the results of Jehovah Rophe's preventative medicine by simply living self-controlled lives. They have not smoked, which has been proven dangerous to health. They have not given themselves to drugs, alcohol or other substances that can shorten one's life span. Demonstrating temperance in many other areas of practice has contributed to the good health of Christians.

A second element of the healing of Jehovah Rophe is corrective medicine. Just as God healed the bitter waters of Marah, He can heal those with disease. Within a few years of this promise to Moses, his sister Miriam was healed of leprosy (see Num. 12:11-16). Today, Jehovah Rophe still heals—physically, mentally, socially and spiritually.

The tree cast into the waters at Marah may be taken as a symbol of the cross of Jesus Christ. which in turn symbolizes God's ultimate healing power. While physical healing may not immediately come to everyone who embraces the Atonement (in some cases it may not be realized until the Resurrection; see 1 Cor. 15:42), the cross stands for any healing relationship God has with man. The apostle Paul reminds, "Cursed *is* every one that hangeth on a tree" (Gal. 3:13), indicating that Christ took the curse of human infirmities upon Himself.

The miracles of modern science have not yet invented a cure for the common cold. Yet the mother who bundles up her children before sending them out into the snow is exercising preventative medicine. If they do catch cold, or the flu, she gives them corrective medicine such as cough syrup or aspirin. In much the same way, Jehovah Rophe bundles us up in His love and tells us how to live a righteous life, thus giving us preventative measures to keep us physically and spiritually healthy. And when we do fall into sickness or sin, He has corrective medicine. Sometimes this is in the form of the forgiveness of sins. At other times He grants miraculous physical healing. At still other times He restores a relationship or heals a psychological problem. He is Jehovah Rophe, The LORD [Our] Healer.

Righteousness: *Jehovah Tsidkenu*

God is also Jehovah Tsidkenu, "The LORD Our Righteousness," meeting our desperate need to have the guilt of sin removed. It is Jehovah Tsidkenu who "leadeth me in the paths of righteousness" (Ps. 23:3).

Sin is many things, among them seeking our own way or straying like wayward sheep from the right path. "We have turned every one to his own way" (Isa. 53:6). When our ways are the ways of sin, we are guilty of transgression. We deserve the judgment or punishment of hell. But Jehovah Roi, our Shepherd who guides us, is also Jehovah Tsidkenu, The LORD Our Righteousness, who in mercy will give us a new standing before Him.

The phrase Jehovah Tsidkenu is found in Jeremiah 23:6. When the Lord returns at the end of the age, the Jews who have rejected Jesus Christ will recognize Him as their Messiah and turn to Him as their Savior. Jeremiah predicts that they will then come to know God by the name The LORD Our Righteousness. It is through His righteousness that the Jews will come to know the justification that Christians already experience.

Justification is not being made inherently righteous, but *declared* righteous through the righteousness of Christ. A right standing before God is not something we can gain for ourselves. God must declare us righteous. Therefore it is Jehovah Tsidkenu who "leadeth me in the paths of righteousness" (Ps. 23:3). He declares His own to be righteous not because of what we have done but "for his name's sake" (v. 3).

Courage: *Jehovah Nissi*

"Though I walk through the valley of the shadow of death, I will fear no evil" (Ps. 23:4). This courage that conquers our fears comes from Jehovah Nissi, "The LORD My Banner."

Fear often comes when we face the unknown, or feel overwhelmed by opposing forces. The small boy, afraid of the dark, wants his mother to go upstairs with him when he goes to bed. A man walking down a dark road at night wants a companion. Many other fears beset us. But when we know Jehovah Nissi, The LORD My Banner, we can walk with courage and the confidence of victory.

The phrase, Jehovah Nissi, was a battle term. The soldier who became separated from his outfit in conflict needed to be able to find his army's battle staff or flag flying above the conflict. He could rally to the flag and not fight alone. Hence, Jehovah Nissi, The LORD My Banner.

This title was revealed when Israel went to battle with Amalek. This was Israel's first fight after escaping from Egypt. Throughout the Old Testament, Israel had a continuing war with Amalek. Joshua led the troops into battle at Rephidim, while Moses stood on top of a hill with the rod of God in his hand. As long as Moses held up his hands (in prayer?) Israel prevailed; but "When he let down his hand, Amalek prevailed" (Exod. 17:11). When Moses' hands became tired, Aaron and Hur held his hands up so he could continue to intercede. As a result, Joshua won the day. "And Moses built an altar, and called the name of it Jehovah-nissi" (v. 15). This is another name given to

God by man. The LORD My Banner means, "the LORD that prevaileth." Even though men fought the battle, God gave the victory.

Amalek serves as a symbol for the flesh in the Old Testament. Even today, Christians battle the flesh, struggling with their old nature. It is God who gives us the victory in this battle, too—a victory that is already guaranteed because of the death of Jesus Christ on the cross. Yet the Bible teaches that the Christian must wrestle, run and fight. The Christian can serve the Lord with complete confidence about the outcome of the battle, because Jehovah Nissi, The LORD My Banner, will prevail.

Loneliness: *Jehovah Shammah*

When the psalmist says, "Thou *art* with me" (Ps. 23:4), he is affirming the presence of Jehovah Shammah, "The LORD Is There."

One of our greatest gifts, along with salvation, is the presence of God in our lives. God promised Moses His presence when He charged Moses to lead Israel out of Egypt: "Certainly I will be with thee" (Exod. 3:12). When Jesus gave His disciples the Great Commission, He promised, "Lo, I am with you alway, *even* unto the end of the world" (Matt. 28:20).

The name Jehovah Shammah is found in Ezekiel 48:35. At the end of his prophecy, Ezekiel described the eternal city and said that even in heaven, "The LORD *is* there" (Jehovah Shammah).

When the Shepherd who is with us comforts us with His rod and His staff (see Ps. 23:4), He is protecting us from the enemy. The shepherd used the rod as a club to beat off wild animals. His staff was a crook that assisted sheep in trouble. With it the shepherd could lift a sheep from the water or from a pit. Technically, the word for "comfort" means "to lead." Jehovah Shammah will lead or guide His sheep by using His rod against attackers or His crook to rescue us from trouble.

Sanctification: *Jehovah Mekaddishkhem*

"Thou anointest my head with oil" (Ps. 23:5). Throughout Scripture, oil is used to sanctify things, people and places for God's special use. The basic meaning of the word "sanctify" is "set apart." In the wilderness, after God delivered Israel from Egypt, He gave instructions regarding the building of the Tabernacle and keeping the Sabbath. The question might arise: Are the people of God sanctified or holy enough for God to live among them and meet with them? Jehovah answers, "Verily my sabbaths ye shall keep: for it *is* a sign between me and you throughout your generations; that *ye* may know that I *am* the LORD that doth sanctify you" (Exod. 31:13).

"The LORD that Sanctifies You" is Jehovah Mekaddishkhem. Since we have no holiness by which to sanctify ourselves, God Himself sets us apart in order for us to dwell in His presence. Jehovah Mekaddishkhem alone is able to sanctify.

Oil was used in various ways in Bible times. The shepherd would anoint the heads of the sheep with oil for several reasons. It was a cleansing agent. When a sheep had a filthy sore, the shepherd used oil to clean dirt or filth from the wound. Similarly, when we sin and receive a wound in our soul, Jehovah Mekaddishkhem cleanses with the oil of His Spirit.

Medicinal oil also heals, just as God anoints us with the healing flow of the blood of Christ in the forgiveness of sins. And oil soothes. When we are sunburned, we put oil or lotion on to take away the burning. Oil replenishes the natural body oils burned away by the sun. When a shepherd anoints the sheep with oil, he replenishes their bodies' natural system.

Oil is a symbol of the Holy Spirit (see 1 Sam. 16:13; Isa. 61:1; Acts 10:38). In the heat of life, Jehovah Mekaddishkhem sends the Third Person of the Trinity to restore, cleanse, soothe and heal.

Jesus Is Jehovah Roi

Jesus Gives a Shepherd's Care

Just as the shepherd gives the sheep his total care and concern, Jesus promised that as the Good Shepherd, He "giveth His life for the sheep" (John 10:11). Because of His dedication to our care, Jesus could say, "I am the good shepherd" (v. 11).

As the Good Shepherd, Jesus knows His "own sheep" so personally that "He calleth his own sheep by name" (v. 3). "He putteth forth his own sheep, he goeth before them, and the sheep follow him" (v. 4). The intimate relationship between shepherd and sheep is a reflection of the relationship between Jesus and the believer. Once a believer enters into the shepherd-sheep relationship, he has eternal life. There he is promised "life...more abundantly" (v. 10).

Shepherding Ministries Under Christ

The word for pastor in the New Testament also means shepherd. A pastor shepherds the souls of those under his care. As a shepherd, the pastor leads the sheep—by example, decision-making and problem-solving. He feeds the sheep—by instruction, counsel and educational administration. He tends the sheep—by discipleship, warning and inspection.

If the pastor is a shepherd, the Sunday School teacher and group leader are extensions of the pastoral ministry into the lives of those in the Sunday School class and small group study. In this way the Sunday School teacher and group leader are also shepherds. Everything the pastor/shepherd is to the larger flock, the teacher and leader are to the Sunday School and small group flocks.

Although Jesus is the Good Shepherd, He communicates His intimate care to us through human shepherds who minister in His name (see John 21:15-17; Acts 20:32; 1 Pet. 5:1-5).

CHAPTER 3

◆ ALMIGHTY GOD ◆

The God Who Supplies My Needs

SOMETIMES we let a problem become a giant crisis. Only later in life do we see how small the original problem really was, especially to the Lord who solves our problems. He is *El Shaddai*, the One strong enough to help and sensitive enough to care.

When I graduated from Dallas Theological Seminary in May 1958, I was also pastoring Faith Bible Church in Dallas at the same time. While I was preaching on the Sunday morning of my Baccalaureate service, someone broke into my house and stole my suits, shirts and my graduation cap and gown. Since the gown was in a suit box, they probably thought it was another suit.

I discovered my loss at about 12:30 P.M. I realized that I couldn't march in the Baccalaureate procession that afternoon. When I phoned the seminary's registrar, he told me I would graduate, of course, but that I couldn't have the honor of marching across the platform. It was a crushing loss to me at the time. I prayed. The registrar phoned back with an idea. I was able to borrow a graduation cap and gown from Southern Methodist University, which had them on hand.

GOD OF NOURISHMENT AND POWER

This scene is typical of the nature of El Shaddai. God was sensitive to my cry, and He was strong enough to supply the answer to my problem.

When the patriarch Abraham was 99 years old, he needed reassurance of what God had promised—that his descendants would become a great nation, that he would inherit the Promised Land and that from him all the nations of the world would be blessed. Abraham had not sought these promises from God. The LORD had appeared to Abraham and given him these promises when he was 75

> *Strength and tenderness...*
> *is a picture of blue jeans...*
> *and lace....We pray to the*
> *Almighty...who is strong...and*
> *to the tender God who weeps*
> *with us....God is both blue*
> *denim and lace.*

years old. But now, in their old age, Abraham and his wife Sarah were past the age to bear children.

A New Name Revealed

God was sensitive to Abraham's need, and strong enough to do something about it. The LORD appeared to him and said, "I *am* the Almighty God [El Shaddai]: walk before me and be thou perfect" (Gen. 17:1). This is the first time that the name Almighty is used in the Bible. It is a compound name consisting of *El*, a shortened form of *Elohim*, the strong Creator; and *Shaddai*, the Hebrew word for Almighty. Even though Shaddai and the Hebrew word for *shad*, meaning breast (as in Gen. 49:25; Job 3:12; Ps. 22:9) are two different words, they sound alike. The wordplay reminds us that God tenderly provides for us. God does not come to Abraham as the Creator alone, but as the God who can supply Abraham's need—as a woman satisfies the need of a child at her breast.

Thus, two divine qualities are implied in the name El Shaddai. God is both the strong One who is able to deliver, and the tender One who nourishes and satisfies. Unfortunately, the English word Almighty tends to communicate only the aspect of God's strength and power. Some feel that the term "All-sufficient" would be a better translation.

How can we communicate both strength and tenderness? It is a picture of blue jeans (toughness) and lace (delicate fabric "tatted" with tenderness). When we have financial needs, we pray to the Almighty, the God who is strong to supply our needs; but we may also cry out to the tender God who weeps with us in our needs. God is both blue denim and lace.

When the term Almighty was first used, God wanted to communicate a new side of His nature to Abraham. For 24 years Abraham had obeyed God and dwelt in the Promised Land. This new name was given to reveal a new aspect of how the God he had been serving works. The same is true of relationships today. The girlfriend may soon be called a sweetheart, a term of endearment. After marriage she is called a wife. Later she may be called Mother.

A New Promise Given

God not only revealed to Abraham a new name, Almighty God; He gave Abraham a new promise: "I will make my covenant between me and thee, and will multiply thee exceedingly" (Gen. 17:2). When God promises His blessings to us, we must claim them and act on them. Abraham was no different. "And Abram fell on his face: and God talked with him" (v. 3). Abraham had to pray, intercede and trust the Almighty for the promise.

God said to Abraham, "As for Sarai thy wife, thou shalt not call her name Sarai, but Sarah *shall* her name be. And I will bless her, and give thee a son also of her: yea, I will bless her, and she shall be *a mother* of nations; kings of people shall be of her" (vv. 15,16).

This, too, was a promise of the Almighty God (El Shaddai). Abraham and Sarah would supernaturally have a son when they were past ordinary child-bearing age. The twofold aspect of the name Almighty God is *strength* and *satisfaction*. Abraham and Sarah would have strength to conceive a son, and this would bring them satisfaction at the fulfillment of God's promise.

THE PROMISE PASSED ON

Abraham passed his knowledge of El Shaddai on to Isaac, the son of promise. For when Isaac was old, he sent his own son Jacob to the land of his ancestors to get a wife, saying, "God Almighty [El Shaddai] bless thee, and make thee fruitful, and multiply thee" (28:3).

The name El Shaddai continued to be handed down in the family. When Jacob grew to be an old man, he in turn blessed his own son Joseph in the name of "The Almighty, who shall bless thee with blessings" (49:25).

The name Almighty God occurs 48 times in the Old Testament. Of these occurrences, 31 are in the book of Job. Job lost all his earthly possessions, including his family. He lost his health and ended up sitting on an ash heap and scraping the boils on his body with broken pottery. Job and his friends knew that it is the tough-but-tender Almighty God who can deliver him from his distress, and he was counseled, "Happy is the man whom God correcteth: therefore despise not thou the chastening of the Almighty" (5:17).

From the book of Job we learn that the tender, caring Almighty God also has a stern aspect to His personality. Even though a mother loves her children, she will correct and spank if necessary, because she loves them. A loving mother will put soothing ointment on a burn, but she will also spank a child who plays near the fire. She doesn't spank because she is angry, but because she loves her child and wants him to learn not to lie near the fire. In the same manner the Almighty may chasten His children both as the strong One and as tender Father. In love He will soothe our wounds, but also in love He may allow us to be wounded if necessary for our discipline.

In the New Testament, the name Almighty (Grk. *pantokrator*) occurs 12 times, 9 of them in the book of Revelation. The same tough and tender sides of God's nature are revealed here in the use of the name Almighty. The Almighty will faithfully reward the believer for good works; and He will pour out judgment on the willful unbeliever. He is eternal: "I am Alpha and Omega, the beginning and the ending, saith the Lord, which is, and which was, and which is to come, the Almighty" (Rev. 1:8).

El Shaddai, the Almighty God, is a name that believers should know and trust. When we face problems or dangers we can call on the Almighty for help. He will not always take away our problems or remove us from life's storms, but He will give us the strength to endure them. We should remember three things about problems: We can't run from them; we can't prevent their coming into our lives; and we can't always solve all of them. Yet El Shaddai strengthens us in the midst of problems.

James counseled: "Count it all joy when you fall into various trials" (Jas. 1:2, *NKJV*). He explains that (1) trials or tests are inevitable, (2) they are "various" or different and (3) they need not defeat us, but can actually be met with joy. As the child of God faces trouble, he must remember that the world is not coming to an end because he can't solve all problems. Nor is he a failure. All of God's children have problems.

APPLICATION

Six guidelines, each one related to the character of El Shaddai, will help believers face and overcome problems:

1. Separate yourself from sin (negative holiness). Many of our problems come because of sin in our lives. It is the nature of sin to defeat, destroy, disrupt, dilute and damage the child of God. Therefore, the Almighty insists on the principle of separation from sin: "Come out from among them, and be ye separate...touch not the unclean *thing*...ye shall be my sons and daughters, saith the Lord Almighty" (2 Cor. 6:17,18). El Shaddai is still both strong to save and tender to help. But if we harbor sin in our lives, He cannot be merely tender and kind; He must judge.

2. Seek El Shaddai's presence (positive holiness). The Almighty is tender, and wants to help His children, but He wants us to actively seek Him. I sometimes see a ministerial student struggling in seminary with finances. He works a job, goes to seminary where he struggles to learn Hebrew and Greek, and he preaches at every opportunity. When he prays for help, especially for financial relief, usually God does not send a rich benefactor to pay the student's way. If the seminarian had an easy life, he would probably not seek help from the Almighty, and his effectiveness as a minister would be hampered. El Shaddai asks him to work hard, to actively pursue His presence in order to have an effective ministry.

When we reach heaven and stand around the throne, we will sing, "Holy, holy, holy, Lord God Almighty" (Rev. 4:8). Then we will experience the all-sufficient, holy God of strength and satisfaction—all of which is attached to Him in the name El Shaddai.

3. Rest in the presence of El Shaddai. God is not just a powerful Creator who is far removed from believers. He is as close as a mother or a shepherd. Once there was a wayward sheep who kept wandering from the flock. The shepherd knew the dangers. The wayward sheep might fall off a ledge or drown in a swift current. But no matter how many times the shepherd tenderly brought back the sheep, it would stray again. Finally, for the sheep's own good, it was time for toughness. The shepherd broke one of the sheep's legs, and it was forced to stay near the shepherd in safety. "He that dwelleth in the secret place of the most High shall abide under the shadow of the Almighty [Shaddai]" (Ps. 91:1).

4. Follow the directions of El Shaddai. A child cannot dwell in the favor of his parents without obeying each parent's voice. Because we are born in sin, it is difficult to obey. We like to do things our own way. A mother tried to get her young son to sit down, but he would not. Finally, she forcibly made him sit. He said, "I may be sitting down on the outside, but inside I'm standing up."

The boy is a picture of too many believers. Instead of obeying from the heart, we rebel inside. When God came to Abraham He had to remind him, "I *am* the Almighty God [El Shaddai]; walk before me, and be thou perfect" (Gen. 17:1).

5. Evaluate your spiritual health. If you do not sense that God is using hardships in your life to move you closer to Him or to reveal unconfessed sin, it may indicate that you aren't really His child. The writer of Hebrews says, "If ye endure chastening, God dealeth with you as with sons: for what son is he whom the father chasteneth not?" (12:7; see also vv. 5-11). It is the nature of El Shaddai to lovingly discipline those who are really His children. Hence, "My son, despise not thou the chastening of the Lord...For whom the Lord loveth he chasteneth, and scourgeth every son whom he receiveth" (vv. 5,6).

In the book of Ruth, we read of Naomi and her husband Elimelech. Both disobeyed God and left Israel, where there was a famine, to live in Moab, which was prospering. They made their choice with an eye on *things* rather than with the eye of faith. They prospered in Moab, but Elimelech died. Then both of Naomi's sons died. Finally, when everything was stripped from her, Naomi returned to Israel and her hometown. She told her friends, "Call me not Naomi [pleasant], call me Mara [bitterness]...seeing the LORD hath testified against me, and the Almighty [Shaddai] hath afflicted me" (Ruth 1:20,21).

The Almighty disciplines His disobedient children. If you have ever been punished by a loving parent, you know that there can be comfort even in the pain of judgment. In the same way, you can take comfort in the midst of discipline from the fact that you are a child of God. If you will obey the Almighty, He will be your shaddai—your strength and satisfaction.

6. Claim the provision of El Shaddai. Because God is faithful and strong to save, He will take care of you. When ministerial students come to seminary, I always challenge them with the promise, "Faithful *is* he that calleth you, who also will do it" (1 Thess. 5:24). I point out to students that if God has called them, they can endure the problems of seminary such as time pressure, heavy studies, Greek and Hebrew, money, etc. "God will do it," I promise the students. And some students have told me 20 years later that it was this promise that got them through seminary and into the ministry. He who calls us in His divine tenderness will hear our cry in His divine strength.

When old Jacob was facing death, he wanted to bless his grandsons, and He wanted them to walk in obedience to God. So he gave them the promise of El Shaddai: "The Almighty who shall bless thee with blessings" (Gen. 49:25). Jacob, who had experienced both the blessings and the punishment of El Shaddai, knew that these two aspects of His nature would guide his grandchildren as they followed the LORD.

CHAPTER 4

❖ MOST HIGH GOD ❖

Possessor of Heaven and Earth

A wife may call her husband "Honey," usually reflecting their intimate relationship. An enemy, however, would use an entirely different name. What names would the enemies of God use when addressing Him?

When Satan and his demons, God's prime enemies, address Him, they usually use the term *El Elyon*, which means Most High God. They do not use this name to curse God or to impugn His character. Rather, they call Him Most High God because that title reflects the attributes of God they lust after.

THE SUPERLATIVE GOD

As we have seen, the prefix El comes from *Elohim*, "strong Creator." Elyon is "highest" or "most." It is the superlative degree, as in high, higher and highest. Elyon means that the Lord is "God of gods" or "the ultimate God."

The superlative word *elyon* is used in the book of Ezekiel to speak of the highest pool, the highest gate, the highest porch and the highest house. The heavens are higher than the earth (comparative) but God is highest (superlative). The term reveals that God is the highest, and that everyone else is below Him. Because God is Elyon, He has the power to rule and the right to receive worship from all below Him.

When the title El Elyon first appears in Scripture, (see heading "Melchizedek Served El Elyon"), the *King James Version* identifies it with Him who is "possessor of heaven and earth" (Gen. 14:19). One church father translated this phrase "founder of heaven and earth," and the *New International Version* speaks of the "creator" of heaven and earth. El Elyon is a name for God that is often associated with His creation, revealing that He is both sovereign and owner of the heaven and the earth.

The word translated "possessor" in Genesis 14:19 is a derivative of a verb from which the *King James Version* on other occasions has rendered "possess" and "contain." Another form means "whole." Therefore to possess heaven and earth is to have a rightful claim to the ownership of all there is. When Abraham tells the king of Sodom, "I have lifted up mine hand unto...the most high God [El Elyon], the possessor of heaven and earth" (14:22), he is telling this Gentile leader that God is his leader and he is God's servant. Abraham is declaring that the king had received everything from God and will give everything back to God.

In the New Testament, Stephen's sermon to the unbelieving Jews proclaimed that God was not limited to their Jewish Temple: "The most High dwelleth not in temples made with hands" (Acts 7:48). Stephen's point was that God did not always limit Himself to a man-made temple, so the new, emerging Church would not be limited to the Old Testament Temple. If Stephen had used the name *Jehovah*, he would have linked God to the Temple; but the name El Elyon identified the Church with the world, which was the target of the Great Commission.

The name El Elyon is also often identified with the Gentiles (i.e., the earth) rather than the Jews (i.e., the Promised Land). This usage appears in the book of Deuteronomy: "the most High divided to the nations [i.e., Gentiles] their inheritance, when he separated the sons of Adam" (32:8).

Satan Knows of El Elyon's Power

Satan knows there are armies on this earth and armies in heaven. These armies are made up of angels, called "sons of God" or His "ministers." Angels are beings with intellect, emotion and will. These beings rejoiced at Creation (see Job 38:7). They appeared before the presence of God (see 1:6; 2:1). Angels are higher than man (comparative), but God is the highest being (superlative), greater than both angels and people.

Satan knows and lusts after power. He knows there are powers on the earth, that the powers of angels in heaven are higher (comparative) and that the power of God is highest (superlative). Satan and his demons are great in power, too (see Eph. 6:12), but God's power is the greatest of all. He is El Elyon. Whereas evil men on this earth are blinded to the existence and power of God, evil angels and Satan know God as the Most High God. Thus, El Elyon is the "God of gods" (Ps. 136:2), the "King of kings" and the "Lord of lords" (Rev. 19:16).

Before the fall of Adam and Eve, Lucifer (Satan or the devil) referred to God as the "most High" (Isa. 14:14). Lucifer, the first created angel, was in rebellion against God. He was not just trying to destroy God, but to take God's place. In Isaiah 14:12-14, Satan, who is prefigured in the king of Babylon (see v. 4), exercises his self-will in assaulting the authority of God and attempting to take His place. Satan said:

1. "I will ascend into heaven."
2. "I will exalt my throne."
3. "I will sit also upon the mount of the congregation."
4. "I will ascend above the heights of the clouds."
5. "I will be like the most High [El Elyon]."

As Satan climbed these five steps toward the place of God, his ultimate passion was to be like God and sit in God's place. When Satan surveyed the heavens created by God, he wanted them. But more than wanting to possess things, he wanted to be God. Therefore, Satan called God the Most High God, the position he desired for himself.

In the New Testament, the name Most High God is used by fallen angels (demons) when addressing Jesus Christ.

When a demon recognizes the presence of Jesus Christ, he cannot help but confess His deity. What a shame that...many Christians are tongue-tied...when it comes to confessing Jesus Christ!

Legion, the fallen angel who had possessed the man of Gadara said, "Jesus, thou Son of the most high God" (Mark 5:7). The demon recognized what the New Testament teaches, "All things were made by him [Jesus]; and without him was not any thing made that was made" (John 1:3) And again, "All things were created by him, and for him: and he is before all things, and by him all things consist" (Col. 1:16, 17).

Demons recognized Paul as a preacher of Jesus Christ. A demon-possessed servant girl followed Paul and his company throughout Philippi crying out, "These men are the servants of the Most High God" (Acts 16:17, *NKJV*). When a demon recognizes the presence of Jesus Christ, he cannot help but confess His deity. What a shame that, in comparison, many Christians are tongue-tied or mute when it comes to confessing Jesus Christ!

On other occasions, demons recognized Christ as, "the Holy One of God" (Mark 1:24), even though they did not link Him to the Most High. Again in the book of Acts, there was an exorcist service when a person attempted to cast out a demon. The evil spirit answered and said, "Jesus I know, and Paul I know; but who are ye?" (19:15). Again, demons indicated that they knew Christ. This is reinforced by James who said, "Thou believest that there is one God; thou doest well: the devils also believe, and tremble" (Jas. 2:19).

Why do demons and Satan recognize the Most High God and Jesus? Because they want to be who He is (the Founder or Creator) and they want to possess what is His (the heavens and the earth).

MELCHIZEDEK SERVED EL ELYON

Although Satan was the first to use the name El Elyon, before the Creation of the world (see lesson notes on Isa. 14:12-14), the first reference in the Scriptures as we have them is by Abraham, in Genesis 14:17-24. Abraham, the man of faith, pursued a band or army of raiders to Damascus to rescue his nephew, Lot. Abraham divided his 318 servants and attacked the enemy by night. The Bible describes the victory as "the slaughter of Chedorlaomer" (v. 17). Abraham not only brought back Lot, but the goods and the people that were with him as well. Abraham apparently was a fierce and skillful warrior, but the sovereign God and His intervention gave Abraham the victory.

On his return from the battle, Abraham came near the

ancient city of Salem, which later will be called Jerusalem. He met two kings in the "valley of Shaveh," which was also called "the king's dale" (v. 17)—apparently a place where the king met dignitaries for certain ceremonies. This is probably the brook Kidron, between Gethsemane and the Golden Gate to the Temple.

The two kings approached Abraham in this cool, green valley. They were kings of city-states, meaning each man was like the mayor of a great city, ruling over those within his walled city, plus those in the immediately surrounding area.

The first king was from Sodom, which had been plundered in the raid in which Lot was captured. This was the evil city known for its sodomy, which God would later destroy. When Abraham and Lot divided up the land, Lot had gone to live in Sodom, choosing the well-watered plains that surrounded the city (see 13:8-12). He chose with the outward eye, not the inward voice of God. He did not recognize that he was vulnerable to: (1) An attack from marauding armies as they plundered the Jordan valley; and (2) the attack of Satan who would attempt to destroy his morality through sodomy.

Now the king of Sodom wanted to strike a bargain with Abraham. The rules of war said that Abraham, the victor, could keep the people and possessions he had captured. But the king of Sodom said, "Give me the persons, and take the goods unto thyself" (14:21). The deal was simple. The king of Sodom, with the worldly man's practical eye to the value of material goods, would make Abraham a rich man with the goods from Sodom.

But the second king, Melchizedek, king of Salem ("King of peace"—see Heb. 7:2) had a different set of values. Melchizedek was not only a king; he was also a priest of El Elyon (see Gen. 14:18,19). It is natural that this priest-king would call God by this name, since it was associated with the Gentiles. The remarkable thing about the story is that Abraham, father of the chosen people, actually paid tithes of the booty he had won to Melchizedek the Gentile (see v. 20).

Some have thought that this is a Christophany—an appearance of Christ—and that Melchizedek was in fact Jesus. The writer of the book of Hebrews does compare Melchizedek to Christ, who is said to be a priest "after the order of Melchizedek" (see Heb. 5:6; Ps. 110:4). But it is likely that the biblical writers were only drawing an analogy between the two figures.

What is more likely is that in this story two great men meet—a weary Abraham returning from a long trip and a hard battle, and a dignified Gentile king who is also a believer in El Elyon. Melchizedek served bread and wine to Abraham in gratitude for protecting his city, Salem, and for any possessions that were returned to him. In exchange, Abraham gave Melchizedek a tithe of what he had gained, just as today tithes are given to churches for God's use. Note that Abraham did not worship Melchizedek, but Melchizedek's God, El Elyon. As Abraham himself said, "I have lift up mine hand unto the LORD, the most high God, the possessor of heaven and earth" (Gen. 14:22).

DANIEL AND THE POWER OF GOD MOST HIGH

The next extensive use of the name El Elyon is found in the book of Daniel (see 3:26; 4:17,24,25,32). Because El Elyon is identified with the Gentiles, it is only natural for Daniel, a young Hebrew boy who was taken captive into Babylon, to pray to God who possessed the heavens and the earth.

In fact, it is interesting that Daniel did not rely heavily on Jewish-related names for God. Besides El Elyon, Daniel's next favorite name for deity was "the God of heaven" (2:19). Why did he use these names? Because he was (1) outside the Promised Land, (2) he realized that the Temple was destroyed, (3) Gentiles controlled Israel and (4) Gentiles controlled Daniel's own circumstances. Therefore Daniel prayed to the One who possessed heaven and earth—the God who is Lord over Babylon as well as Israel, and who is greater than any earthly circumstance.

When Nebuchadnezzar, king of Babylon, had a terrible dream and no one could interpret it, Daniel came to the palace and through the power of El Elyon was able to give the interpretation (see 2:1-45). As a result, the heathen king of Babylon recognized El Elyon as Daniel's God. But since He was not the king's God, Nebuchadnezzar made an idol of gold approximately 90 feet tall and commanded everyone to bow down and worship it (see 3:1-7; many think the idol was Nebuchadnezzar himself, and people were worshiping him as an expression of deity).

Shadrach, Meshach and Abednego, three other Jews in Babylon, refused to worship the idol. King Nebuchadnezzar cast them into a fiery brick kiln, called a furnace in the Bible (see vv. 8-23). When Nebuchadnezzar looked into the mouth of the brick kiln to see their fate, he saw four men walking—Shadrach, Meshach and Abednego, plus a fourth person who is described thus: "The form of the fourth is like the Son of God" (v. 25).

Nebuchadnezzar shouted into the mouth of the fiery brick kiln, "Ye servants of the most high God [El Elyon] come forth, and come hither" (v. 26). It is remarkable that this Gentile king, who was the most powerful man in the world and who might be expected to identify *himself* as the possessor of the earth, identified God by that title, using His Gentile name.

But even though Nebuchadnezzar *recognized* God, he did not worship Him. In fact, in the next chapter, the king walked through his city boasting and taking credit for all the grandeur of ancient Babylon (see 4:29,30). Nebuchadnezzar put himself in the place of God.

Daniel saw in a vision what was coming. He predicted the fall of Nebuchadnezzar from power, as a result of his arrogance, "till thou know that the most High [El Elyon] ruleth in the kingdom of men and giveth it to whomsoever he will" (v. 25). He delivered the bad news to King Nebuchadnezzar in the name of El Elyon: "This is the interpretation, O king, and this *is* the decree of the most High, which is come upon my lord the king" (v. 24).

The decree happened just as Daniel said. Nebuchadnezzar's mind was taken from him. He was apparently struck with lycanthropy—commonly called the wolf-man disease. He went out into the fields, behaving like an animal. He ate grass like an ox, and his hair grew to look like a beast's. He lost his mind for seven years, and, in the process, lost his authority over his realm (see vv. 25,26,28,31-33). The possessor of heaven and earth does not share His glory with anyone—even the king of Babylon.

At the end of seven years, Nebuchadnezzar came to his senses, regained his throne and his life returned to normal (see v. 36). After his experience he could finally confess, "I blessed the most High, and I praised and honored him that liveth for ever, whose dominion is an everlasting dominion, and his kingdom is from generation to generation" (v. 34; see also v. 37).

Daniel also used the name Most High God (El Elyon)

when dealing with the next heathen ruler of Babylon, King Belshazzar (see 5:18). It was King Belshazzar who took the gold vessels which had been captured from Solomon's Temple and used them in a drunken feast (see vv. 1-4). Suddenly a hand came and wrote upon the wall "Mene, mene, tekel, upharsin" (5:5,25).

Upon seeing the hand, Belshazzar cried out, fearing for his life. The queen mother (the wife of Nebuchadnezzar) was called to the palace. She indicated that Daniel could interpret what Belshazzar had seen (see vv. 10-14). When Daniel came to confront Belshazzar, he reminded him, "O thou king, the most high God [El Elyon], gave Nebuchadnezzar thy father a kingdom, and majesty, and glory and honor" (v. 18).

The Most High God once again showed that it is He alone who possesses the heavens and the earth. That very night Belshazzar was slain, and power was transferred to Darius the Mede (see vv. 30,31).

OTHER GLIMPSES OF EL ELYON

Toward the end of his life, Moses ascribes to El Elyon the sovereign power to set the boundaries of the nations, as we have seen. "When the Most High divided to the nations their inheritance, when he separated the sons of Adam, he set the bounds of the people according to the number of the children of Israel" (Deut. 32:8). Again, we see that it is El Elyon, not mere man, who really possesses the heavens and the earth.

On several occasions David prayed to El Elyon, the Most High God. In Psalm 9:2 David exulted, "I will sing praise to thy name, O thou most High." The writer of Psalm 91 gives testimony, "He that dwelleth in the secret place of the most High shall abide under the shadow of the Almighty" (v. 1).

Applications of El Elyon

What lessons can Christians draw from the way the name El Elyon is used in Scripture?

The Satanic Substitute

Satan has a twofold desire: (1) To rebel against everything that is holy and godly; and (2) to substitute himself in the place of God as "possessor of heaven and earth." This is in accordance with the New Testament picture of the Antichrist, who not only opposes Christ but wants to be a substitute Christ. Satan regrets that he cannot be the founder of heaven and earth; the world is already created. So he wants to be the possessor of all that is, and to have people worship him instead of El Elyon.

When Satan tempted Jesus Christ to fall down and worship him, he offered the kingdoms of this world in exchange (see Matt. 4). As the god of this world (see Eph 2:2,3; 6:11,12), Satan wants to possess it. And he wanted Jesus to recognize his claim.

The Process Principle

As we have seen, demons recognize El Elyon and are forced to cry out that fact in acknowledgment (see Mark 5:7). Demons want to possess the world, and they want to possess people. But how do demons possess a person as they possessed Legion and the young girl who told fortunes? (see Mark 5:9; Acts 16:16-18). Demon possession comes slowly. Just as God wants to fill a person with the Holy Spirit (see Eph. 5:18), so Satan wants to fill a person. The *New International Version* of the Bible calls this "demon-possession" (see Matt. 15:22); but the term is actually "demonization" in the original language.

People are demonized in the same way they are filled

with the Spirit: in a gradual process. (1) They yield to the influence. (2) The more they yield and seek, the more they become filled or possessed. (3) Both kinds of spirits usually come gradually, according to the level of learning and commitment. (4) Some are more filled or possessed than others. And (5) both filling and possession are for the purpose of honoring and serving one's master.

The Holy Spirit does not fill a person who is rebellious to God. He comes only with yielding and seeking. In the same way, demons do not invade a person who is not seeking the occult and yielded to satanic powers.

The Jesus Answer
The solution to demon possession is the name Jesus. They already recognize His name and His person. The only power to cast out demons is "in the name of Jesus." His blood is the power that repels them (Acts 20:28; Rev. 1:5). The solution to gradual demon possession is increasing dependence on the name of Jesus.

The Tithing Principle
The tithe was first given when Abraham gave a tenth of his spoils to a Gentile, Melchizedek, king of Salem and priest of El Elyon. The tithe is usually a gift to deity. Inasmuch as God possesses heaven and earth, we must surrender everything we have to the control of God. The tithe is only a token of what we possess. Giving a tithe to God is not buying God or bribing Him. A tithe is an outward symbol of the inward gift of oneself to God.

Many claim that tithing was only for God's people under the Old Covenant. They say it is a principle of the Law and should not be used under grace. But inasmuch as the tithe is suggested and used to "bless the Lord," why should anyone do less today? However, God who possesses all things, not only wants our tithe; He wants everything that we have. We give Him all of our love, our hearts, our bodies and our possessions. He controls everything. A tithe is given to God to indicate that all the rest belongs to Him.

The Possession Principle

The Most High God possesses heaven and earth. All Creation belongs to Him because He is its Creator. However, the Most High God wants most to possess our hearts. This includes our will, our feelings and our mind. The proper response to this claim on our lives is (1) to yield to Him; (2) to seek His blessing; and (3) to obey His command.

Neither Satan nor man should expect to possess that which is God's by His divine right. The psalmist said, "When I consider thy heavens....What is man, that thou art mindful of him?" (Ps. 8:3,4). Looking at Creation should only bring us to acknowledge the greatness of El Elyon, not to create a desire to possess it as our own. The same thing is true of life itself. James asked the question, "What *is* your life? It is even a vapor, that...vanisheth away" (Jas. 4:14). Because we are only here for a short time, we realize that we are not our own. The high and holy El Elyon has created us for His own pleasure.

El Elyon and the Name of Jesus

Because God is three-in-one, Jesus Christ is El Elyon. He is the Creator, Sustainer and Possessor of heaven and earth. As glorious as is the name El Elyon, it is the name of Jesus that will be the final name, for "at the name of Jesus, every knee should bow, of *things* in heaven, and *things* in earth, and *things* under the earth; and *that* every tongue should confess that Jesus Christ *is* Lord, to the glory of God the Father" (Phil. 2:10,11).

El Elyon and El Shaddai

The titles El Elyon (Most High God) and El Shaddai (the Almighty) are linked together in Psalm 91:1: "He that dwelleth in the secret place of the most High shall abide under the shadow of the Almighty." These two titles are in juxtaposition, revealing two sides of God at the same time. The powerful El Elyon, who is supreme and omnipotent is also the personal God who is the Fountainhead of all grace. El Elyon is able to do what He wishes because He is powerful; El Shaddai gives grace and mercy. El Elyon causes us to fear and tremble before His greatness; El Shaddai invites us to come for comfort under His wings.

Mighty and gracious—El Elyon and El Shaddai are One God. He is able to do exceeding abundantly above all that we can ask or think because He is El Elyon. He is able to present us faultless before the divine throne because He is El Shaddai.

CHAPTER 5

❖ THE EVERLASTING GOD ❖

The Secret Name of God

WHY do we keep secrets? There are many reasons to conceal information. Sometimes secrets are good, and sometimes they are harmful. A parent keeps a Christmas gift hidden to surprise the children and make Christmas more enjoyable. A poverty-stricken mother doesn't tell her children that there isn't enough food for the next day in order to keep them from worrying. Sometimes, when people are not able to handle the burden of knowledge, it's kind not to tell them everything.

God keeps secrets for many reasons, too. But He never hides things to harm us or out of selfishness. He doesn't let us know how we will die, or when. It might devastate us. He doesn't tell us all the good things He will do, lest we let up and not work as hard.

God doesn't tell us everything about Himself. Some things about His justice might depress us. Some things about His goodness we could not understand because we are not God. Only God can fully understand God.

GOD THE ETERNAL AND MYSTERIOUS

El Olam, the Everlasting God, is a secret name for God, hinting at His mysterious nature. The prefix El, we have noted, is from *Elohim* ("strong Creator"). Olam means time, or age. With a tiny change in the vowel signs in Hebrew, the ancient rabbis spelled it *alam*, "hidden" (see chap. 1), underscoring the mysterious nature of God. God's everlasting or timeless nature—without beginning or end—is one of the most profound mysteries of His nature.

In Psalm 90:2 the psalmist exalts God by saying that "from everlasting [olam] to everlasting, thou *art* God." The Hebrew word olam is a synonym for the Greek word *aion*, meaning age or dispensation. And in Psalm 10:1 the meaning of alam, secret or hidden, is illustrated. The psalmist

---

By calling on God as El Olam, Abraham was calling on the One who is always and eternally available to us....People today need just such a God as the eternal, unchangeable Lord, El Olam.

---

feels estranged from God and asks, "*Why* hidest thou *thyself* in times of trouble?" (see also Lev. 5:2; 2 Kings 4:27).

BEER-SHEBA: PLACE OF REVELATION

The title Everlasting God was first revealed to Abraham at the desert oasis Beer-sheba. The only water at Beer-sheba was a well that Abraham had dug. It was the last well a traveler would pass before entering the desolate Sinai peninsula, making Beer-sheba a strategically located oasis. It had been taken from Abraham violently by the servants of Abimelech, the tribal chieftain of the Philistines. Abraham reproved Abimelech, and out of this confrontation came a covenant of peace. The agreement between Abraham and Abimelech was symbolized by animal sacrifice and accompanied by an oath. Abraham also "planted a grove in Beer-sheba, and called there on the name of the LORD, the everlasting God" (El Olam, Gen. 21:33).

Scholars have attempted to determine why the name El Olam was revealed at this particular time and place. Why was God called the Everlasting God at Beer-sheba, instead of somewhere else? Some have suggested that this is the place where Abraham first exercised squatters rights in the Promised Land. Giving Abraham and his descendants the land of Palestine was a part of the "everlasting [olam] covenant" that God had made with Abraham (17:7). When Abraham dug a well and possessed Beer-sheba, it was an act of faith in God's eternal promise. In calling *Jehovah* El Olam, Everlasting God, Abraham was expressing faith in the God of the everlasting covenant. There is mystery or hiddenness (alam) here, too: It is a mystery that Abraham had faith enough to see the well of Beer-sheba as a down-payment on the future kingdom.

Place of Availability

By calling on God as El Olam, Abraham was calling on the One who is always and eternally available to us. To use modern theological language, he called upon the omniscient, omnipresent and omnipotent God—the God who is eternally changeless. People today need just such a God as the eternal, unchangeable Lord, El Olam. We call on Him because "thy tender mercies and thy lovingkindnesses...have been ever [olam] of old" (Ps. 25:6). David also said that "the LORD is good; his mercy *is* everlasting; and His truth *endureth* to all generations" (100:5). El Olam means "the mercy of the LORD *is* from everlasting to everlasting upon them that fear him, and his righteousness unto children's children" (103:17).

Place of Protection

Thus, when Abraham called upon El Olam at Beer-sheba, he was asking God to protect his well not only as long as Abimelech lived; he sought long-term protection as well. Prior to this event, God had given Abraham immediate help according to his daily need. When he needed protection, wisdom or peace, God was there. But when Abraham calls on El Olam, he is calling for God to protect the Promised Land from the enemies of Abraham's descendants after he died. Abraham wanted Beer-sheba and the Promised Land to be his family inheritance forever.

Place of Mystery

Others see the hidden (alam) God at Beer-sheba. They point out that since the future was hidden (alam) from Abraham, he called on the name of the God who can mysteriously see into future ages (olam). As the apostle Paul teaches, these Old Testament events were shadows or types of what was to come in Christ. For example, the birth of Isaac of a "free woman" and Abraham's rejection of the "son of the bond-maid" is a picture of God's dealing with the Jews and later with the Gentiles (see Gal. 4:22-30). Since these things are done in mystery—i.e., their fulfillment awaits a dispensation (olam) yet to be revealed—they are in the hands of El Olam, the God of secrets and mysteries.

This connection between eternity or age, and mystery, is seen in the way Paul related the idea of a dispensation to mystery:

> If ye have heard of the dispensation of the grace of God which is given me to you-ward: How that

> by revelation he made known unto me the mystery...Which in other ages was not made known unto the sons of men, as it is now revealed unto his holy apostles and prophets by the Spirit (Eph. 3:2, 5).

"Forever" and "hiddenness" are also linked in the Old Testament laws of bondservants. If a slave who was about to go free loved his master and wanted to stay in his service, the law provided that the servant's ear could be pierced with an awl, as a symbol of his choice. It was a sign that he should serve his master "for ever" (olam, Exod. 21:6; Lev. 25:46 indicates that the servitude was only until the year of Jubilee, showing that olam can mean a specific period as well as "everlasting"). In such cases, perhaps God had a secret plan for the slave who made this special commitment.

Similarly, when Hannah gave her child Samuel to the Lord, she said, "*I will not go up* until the child be weaned, and *then* I will bring him, that he may appear before the Lord, and there abide for ever" (1 Sam. 1:22). By this she meant, "as long as he liveth, he shall be lent to the Lord" (v. 28). As it turned out, God had a secret plan for Samuel to carry out in leading Israel to greatness.

The word *olam* is also used to describe a former time. Joshua told his people, "Your fathers dwelt on the other side of the flood in old time" (olam, Josh. 24:2). He did not mean they dwelt there forever, but for a certain time within God's purpose. The word can also refer to this present world, as when the psalmist says, "These are the ungodly, who prosper in the world" (olam, Ps.73:12), meaning they prospered in this present age or in this lifetime. In these references, olam simply expresses the purpose of God in time and does not mean without limits. It shows that God has a purpose in time that is not yet known—it is a mystery. El Olam is "God who has His own purpose in time," or the "God of this time." It implies that God is working His will behind the scenes, and that His purpose will eventually be completed.

We have seen that the name Jehovah is taken from the verb *Hayah*, which means "I am that I am." Jehovah is the God of the present tense. El Olam is the everlasting God, the God of the future, who "will be what I will be."

The New Testament application of El Olam is found in Ephesians 3:8, where Paul speaks of "the unsearchable riches of Christ." God has a secret purpose that we do not know, but it is rich and full of grace. Paul describes how this secret is revealed, "To the intent that now unto the principalities and powers in heavenly *places* might be known by the church the manifold wisdom of God" (v. 10). Only in the New Testament do we see the full explanation of the eternal plan of El Olam, "according to the eternal purpose which he purposed in Christ Jesus our Lord" (v. 11).

There are many complex things in the Bible that transcend our understanding. For example, God seems to have a law respecting the firstborn and the firstfruits. In His mysterious wisdom, He chose Isaac instead of Esau through whom to fulfill His promise to Abraham (see Rom. 9:13). He chose Ephraim over Manasseh (see Gen. 48:14-17). When we are left to ask why, we can only look to El Olam.

As we study the Scriptures, we see the mysterious periods of time that are often repeated: seven days, seven weeks, seven months, seven years and seven times seven (see Lev. 25:8,9). We read of the seven years of tribulation and the coming periods of time, and we do not understand why time is divided into sevens. Yet El Olam understands the reasons.

Under the Law, a person works six days and then rests one. In the new dispensation, most believers rest on the first day and work for six. Why? This is a secret known to El Olam.

We do not know why the Melchizedekian priesthood came first, nor why God then turned to the Aaronic priesthood after the order of Levi. Later God reimplements the Melchizedekian priesthood, with Christ the priest after the order of Melchizedek. Why? Again, El Olam, the Everlasting God whose name is secret has His own purpose.

APPLICATION

Several applications can be drawn from the revelation of the name El Olam, the Everlasting God whose name is secret.

1. *The secret of God gives new meaning to trusting.* Since believers must walk by faith, we must understand the nature of faith. Faith is affirming what God has said in the Bible. To walk by faith is to obey the principles of the Word of God. Hence, the better a person knows the Scriptures, the better opportunity he has for a successful life of faith. But what about obeying what is unknown? Can we guide our lives by what is secret? This is a tough question.

"The secret *things belong* unto the LORD our God: but those *things which are* revealed belong unto us and to our children for ever, that *we* may do all the words of this law" (Deut. 29:29). This verse establishes that God has withheld some secret things from us. Obviously, God would not harm us or treat us unmercifully. He would not withhold something to punish us. Yet, the secrets of God challenge us to trust Him all the more.

What grounds do we have for trusting the secrets of

God? First, the nature of God. He will always act right and judge right. God cannot go against His righteous nature. Second, the way God has dealt with secrets in the past. The things God withheld in the Old Testament, but revealed in the New Testament, were for our good and the glory of God. Therefore, we can now trust God even in the areas that are hidden from us. Because we have established a positive relationship with Him on what we know, we should proceed to trust Him for the things we do not know.

2. *The silence of God gives new meaning to the voice of God.* The believer learns when God speaks, but he also learns when God does not speak. We hear the voice of God in three ways. First, He speaks through His Word. "God, who at sundry times and in divers manners spake in time past unto the fathers by the prophets, hath in these last days spoken to us by his Son" (Heb. 1:1,2). Second, God speaks through nature. He reveals His power and His personality (godhead) through the Creation (see Rom. 1:18-20). And God speaks through the conscience to tell us of our wrong actions. Like a thermometer, the conscience reveals our condition when we go against God's moral law, "their conscience also bearing witness, and their thoughts the mean while accusing or else excusing one another" (Rom. 2:15).

But what about God's silence? What does this say to us? Sometimes we act as though we expect God to speak when He has already spoken. When a person commits adultery, he doesn't need God to speak and tell him his sexual actions are wrong. God has already told him it is wrong. Some even expect God to strike them dead on the spot when they sin. But God has already judged sin on Calvary, and He will not do it again. If you sin and know better, the silence of God ought to frighten you.

Some Christians want God to make an exception for them in special situations, or to tell them what to do. But

God has spoken in His word; now the Christian must seek the principles in God's Word to find God's will for his life. Since God has spoken in the Word, and the normal voice of God is in the Word, do not seek an abnormal voice of God.

3. *What God withholds gives new meaning to the revelation of God.* God's nature is to reveal Himself, just as the nature of light is to shine. When we speak of the revelation of God, we mean the "self revelation" of God. It is something He does. There is no possibility that any person can uncover God or discover something about God if He does not choose to reveal it.

We know much about God from the Bible. We know He has moral attributes of holiness, love and goodness. He has revealed these to us. But there may be other things about God that He has not revealed. Why? Because we cannot understand them. Since God is so majestic, we can only know those things about Him that a human person can know. We cannot know the things that only deity can know. And what we do know, we know only by the Holy Spirit:

> But as it is written, Eye hath not seen, nor ear heard, neither have entered into the heart of man, the things which God hath prepared for them that love Him. But God hath revealed *them* unto us by His Spirit: for the Spirit searcheth all things, yea, the deep things of God (1 Cor. 2:9,10).

4. *We are only responsible for what we know about God.* What we know about God is revealed to us by the Holy Spirit:

> Now we have received, not the spirit of the world, but the spirit which is of God; that we might know

the things that are freely given to us of God. Which things also we speak, not in the words which man's wisdom teacheth, but which the Holy Ghost teacheth; comparing spiritual things with spiritual. But the natural man receiveth not the things of the Spirit of God: for they are foolishness unto him: neither can he know *them*, because they are spiritually discerned (vv. 12-14).

We are not responsible for what we do not know. But the principle of The Burden of Knowledge tells us that we must respond to God as we know Him, acting on the commands we have received, and that we will be judged by our light (understanding).

A great man's statement could be paraphrased, "It is not the things about the Bible I do not understand that bother me—it is the things I understand."

CHAPTER 6

❖ MIGHTY GOD ❖

And the Strong Names of God

DURING my college days I led singing for a revival meeting at a small country Presbyterian church outside of Savannah, Georgia. A fierce thunderstorm swept over the area during the service. Suddenly the power line to the church was snapped by a falling limb, and the lights went out. The piano stopped since the accompanist couldn't see the music. Everyone stopped singing.

At first I panicked, then realized that I had to take control of the situation. "This reminds me of a story," I said, speaking loudly over the sound of the rain. The crowd grew still and the pastor went to get an electrician to fix the wire while I continued my story.

"Augustus Toplady walked through a storm like this years ago. The lightning illuminated the sky like tonight, and the thunder rumbled." I didn't need to establish the mood for the story. The little white frame church was whipped by sheets of rain. The people listened to me.

"Can you imagine being on a lonely mountain road in a storm like this one?" I asked. The congregation didn't respond. I continued: "Augustus Toplady was terrified, thinking he would be stranded in the cold rain, and maybe even die from exposure.

"Up ahead, in a flash of lightning, Augustus Toplady saw a massive rock. He knew he could find protection from the rain on the leeward side of the rock. When he got there, he found that the huge boulder had been split by lightning. By crawling into a cleft of the rock, he was protected from both wind and rain. It was as though the rock had been split just for him.

"Toplady began to think of the spiritual applications. *Jesus was the Rock—firm, strong and protective. Yet Jesus was crucified for me, he thought, and a spear split open His side. He was the Rock cleft for me. In Jesus a person is safe from the storms of sin and strife.*

"As the storm passed, Toplady got paper and pencil and

Many people treat God like a good-luck charm....But God's protection begins with a relationship, not a rabbit's foot.

---

wrote these words: 'Rock of Ages, cleft for me, Let me hide myself in Thee.'"[1]

After I finished telling the story to the audience at that revival meeting, I had them sing the words of the song from memory. We sang without the piano. Other songs followed, and we sang for over 45 minutes. The preacher returned, unable to get the lights repaired at the moment, but he went ahead and preached in the darkened auditorium. I don't remember how many were saved that night, but the lights didn't come back on until after the meeting was over.

Afterward, everyone in the community talked about the story of the rock in the storm. People remembered how the crowd sang. That was the event that drew them back every evening during the rest of the revival meeting.

A God for the Storms of Life

The name Rock is only one of several "strength names" for God in the Old Testament. He is also called Mighty God, Strong One, Fortress and The LORD My Strength, among other titles.

These names were not used by the people of God when they needed might in battle. When they faced a powerful enemy or were in danger of being defeated in battle, they were more likely to call on *Jehovah Sabaoth*, The LORD of Hosts, a name referring to God as Lord of the fighting angels. They would use the strength names of God in the spiritual storms of life when they were weak, discouraged or in need of emotional strength.

Perhaps the best known strength name of God is *El Gibbor*, "Mighty God," and the best-known passage in which it appears is a messianic prophecy in the book of Isaiah. Israel was discouraged at the prospects of losing a military conflict. But the nation really needed spiritual revival. God promised them that a Messiah would come and save them, coming as a child through a virgin birth (see Isa. 7:14). Then Isaiah exults,

> For unto us a Child is born, unto us a Son is given; and the government will be upon his shoulder. And His name will be called Wonderful, Counselor, Mighty God [El Gibbor], Everlasting Father, Prince of Peace (Isa. 9:6, *NKJV*).

The term *Gibbor* was first applied to God by Moses when he said, "For the LORD your God is God of gods, and

Lord of lords, a great God, a mighty [gibbor], and a terrible..." (Deut. 10:17).

David speaks of God as "the LORD strong and mighty, the LORD mighty in battle" in Psalm 24:8, a song celebrating military victory. "Gibbor" appears in this verse as an adjective. It is a term that implies exceptional physical strength and agility, and is used frequently of men mighty in battle. El Gibbor speaks of God's might and power. Another Hebrew word for mighty one is *Abir*, which is a term that blends the words for "mighty" and "strong." Interestingly, Abir is used only in conjunction with the names Jacob and Israel. Jacob used the term on his deathbed, referring to the strength of his son Joseph, whose "bow abode in strength, and the arms of his hands were made strong by the hands of the mighty [Abir] *God* of Jacob" (Gen. 49:24; see also Ps. 132:2). Isaiah spoke of "the mighty One of Israel" (Isa. 1:24).

It is also interesting that Jacob should refer to himself by the name Jacob instead of Israel, the new name God had given to him (Gen. 35:10). The name Jacob means "supplanter" (see 27:36), while Israel means "Prince with God." Apparently Jacob is referring in Genesis 49:24 to his old deceitful ways when he supplanted his brother Esau. But even when he was living after the flesh, "the mighty *God* of Jacob" kept him from falling. He may have been implying that God had been faithful to bring him through the valley of temptation into the place of God's blessing.

Another of the strong names of God is *Tsur*, or "Rock." For those in the Near East traveling near the desert, a rock was noted as a fortress or place of protection. Five times in the song of Moses, God is referred to as a rock (see Deut. 32:4,15,18,30,31). The large rocks in Palestine were so unassailable and enduring that they have impressed man from the beginning of history. When a person was attacked by wild beasts, a rock might be a place of protection and refuge. A rock might provide protection in a storm and shade from the scorching Middle Eastern sun—a need little understood by many Westerners until their soldiers took up posts in the Arabian desert in 1990. The Bible constantly describes the refuge offered by El Gibbor as offering the rest and protection and shade of a great rock.

APPLICATION

Several lessons are apparent when we think of the strong names of God, especially as we compare His strength with ours.

1. *God cannot protect what we won't give Him.* We naturally protect what belongs to us—our "turf," our kids, our job, our homes, our reputation. We don't give nearly so much energy to protecting something that belongs to another. We may try to some degree to help protect someone else's job, and at times we may even go the second mile to defend someone else's property. But we will fight to the death when our own jobs or property is threatened. We work harder, we make twice the calls, we study—and even appeal to a federal fair-employment agency if necessary.

Why do we go to such lengths to protect what is ours? First, because our lives are wrapped up in our work, our relatives, our material possessions. They actually become a part of us. They are an extension of our personality. Second, we are selfish by nature, and we want (lust after) things, people and position. While this is negative motivation, there is also a positive aspect: People and things are the objects of our love. We defend our friends and relatives because we love them. If a school teacher mistreats a child, she usually stirs up the wrath of the mother, who will figuratively (and in some cases literally!) claw the eyes out of anyone who threatens her child.

God loves us and protects us—so much that He gave His Son for us. But sometimes we don't seem to experience that protection. The enemy attacks us like a roaring lion (see 1 Pet. 5:8), and we seem helpless to protect ourselves. We fall into trouble and God seems to stand by. He doesn't rush in to defend us. Why? Because we think that we can protect ourselves, that we are in control of our own lives and property. But God can't protect us when we won't let Him.

The shepherd can protect the sheep who sleeps closest to him. But if a rebellious lamb insists on straying away from the fold at night, it is beyond the shepherd's protection. By removing itself from the fold, the rebellious lamb is prey to predators and other dangers. In the case of the Good Shepherd, such sheep make it difficult for the Mighty God to exercise His power in protecting His own.

God's sheep also make it difficult for Him to protect them in less intentional ways. Some Christians simply fail to surrender their lives to God. They don't deliberately rebel or engage in sins that are visibly outrageous. They just never commit their lives to Jesus Christ. But when troubles come—for example, financial difficulties—they want the protection of the Mighty God. It is fair to ask: Should God protect the finances of believers who never surrender their time, talent or treasures to Him?

Since we are selfish and often blinded to our selfishness, we may be ignorant of the blessings and protection offered by the Mighty God. The child of God may never have surrendered his finances to God and, thus, never experienced His protection in an economic sense. He may not know that God doesn't just want his tithe; He wants it all—not to take it away but to enable the believer to act as

His agent and steward, managing his finances according to divine principles.

2. *God can't work His way in our lives while we work out our ways.* Too often the child of God is fighting his battles his own way. To get victory, the child of God must surrender. This doesn't mean that he becomes passive. Surrendering is just the first step in ceasing self-centered activity. The second step is to fight according to divine principles. God can't protect us with His biblical principles

---

We fall into trouble and God seems to stand by. He doesn't rush in to defend us. Why? Because we think we can protect ourselves.

---

when we stubbornly insist on protecting ourselves with self-seeking principles.

Taking an example from our finances again, a Christian often tries to solve an economic crisis in his own self-seeking determination. He may try moonlighting a second job, push for a raise, put his wife to work, borrow his way out of debt, or try some get-rich-quick scheme. When such measures are tried in our own strength, and when biblical principles are ignored, we are going our own way; there is no room for God to protect His way.

3. *Protection begins with a relationship, not a rabbit's foot.* Many people treat God like a good-luck charm. When facing a difficulty, they use their Bibles like a person rubbing a rabbit's foot—letting it fall open at what he or she hopes will be a lucky passage. But Bible promises are for those who establish a relationship with the God of the Bible. Those who just use it as a lucky charm cannot claim its promises.

God has protected some soldiers on the battlefield who claimed the aid of the Mighty God, but other Christian soldiers have died. What is the difference? The promise of protection (1) must be claimed within the will of God (see Jas. 4:14,15); (2) must be within the realm of what God has promised to protect; and (3) is dependent upon the believer's walk with God. In some cases, believers are not living spiritually in ways that enable them to claim biblical protection.

There are ways to keep ourselves close to the Shepherd so we can expect His protection. First, those who know God's Word can better interpret it and apply it than those who are ignorant of it. Second, those who have a lifelong walk with God are better protected because they have not exposed themselves to danger. For example, the chances of getting lung cancer for practicing Christians who refrain from smoking, would be greatly reduced. Also they would not acquire AIDS from sexual misconduct. They should not go to prison for fraud in reporting their income to the IRS. Salvation does not automatically guarantee healing for the new Christian who is dying from cirrhosis of the liver after being an alcoholic for 30 years.

Those who are living in constant obedience have better reasons to trust in the protection of El Gibbor, the Mighty God. Obviously, the new believer can expect God's immediate acceptance, regardless of his emotional, physical or social condition—just as the prodigal son received the robe, the ring, the welcome-home banquet and the kiss (see Luke 15:11-24). But the new believer cannot expect to avoid the consequences of rebellion against God's laws.

The thief on the cross experienced the consequences of his sins—death on a cross—even though he also enjoyed salvation and the immediate acceptance from Jesus, "Today shalt thou be with me in paradise" (23:39-43).

Note
1. Augustus M. Toplady, *Rock of Ages*, Public domain.

CHAPTER 7

❖ KING ❖

JEHOVAH MELEK

The Throne Name of God

I had a friend who had an audience with the king of Denmark. He told me that when the king entered the room, everyone stopped talking and stood up. "Everyone was aware of his presence," my friend said.

Even though the word *King* (*Melek*) is not actually a personal name of God, it is truly one of His titles. God is the King. The psalmist uses king as a synonym for God: "my King, and my God" (Pss. 5:2; 84:3), equating God with the position and the person of King. When the psalmist says, "For God is my King" (74:12), he is describing God in the function as a ruler. In Psalm 10:16 the psalmist says, "The LORD is King for ever and ever," giving the Lord the title of king.

ISAIAH'S VISION OF THE KING

The prophet Isaiah was called into service after an experience of seeing the LORD as king: "For mine eyes have seen the King, the LORD of hosts" (Isa. 6:5). This call to Isaiah came to him the year that King Uzziah died (see v. 1). Historians believe that Isaiah was a close friend of King Uzziah and that the earthly king had even been Isaiah's hero. King Uzziah had defeated the Philistines, expanded the kingdom and was obviously successful. But when he reached the zenith of power, he apparently felt he could tell God what to do. He intruded into the office of the priesthood, and God struck him with leprosy. Uzziah was rejected from being king, lived in a house separated from everyone and died a leper (see 2 Chron. 26:16-21). With his death, Isaiah's hopes and dreams apparently were dashed. In Isaiah's despondency, God called him to service through a vision of the heavenly King.

Isaiah cried out, "I saw also the Lord sitting upon a throne, high and lifted up, and his train filled the temple" (Isa. 6:1). In this vision, the Lord (*Adonai*, Master) was enthroned in the heavenly throne room, which was apparently a temple, rather than a royal residence like that from which an earthly king might reign. While some commentators believe Isaiah saw the Lord sitting in the earthly Temple, a careful examination reveals that He was more likely sitting in the temple of heaven, the dwelling place of God. His royal robes extended from heaven into the Temple on earth. This was probably a reference to the Shekinah Glory cloud that extended from heaven into the holy of holies.

God the King is also identified as "The LORD of hosts, which dwelleth *between* the cherubim" (1 Sam. 4:4). This was the name used to describe God sitting in the holy of holies on the mercy seat above the Ark of the Covenant. The Lord is the King, but His reign begins in the Temple where there is redemption, rather than from a human throne that is characterized by authority and might. The Lord's righteous reign begins with salvation.

Around the throne of God were seraphim (angels) who are associated with the protection and glory of God. In Isaiah's vision they cried, "Holy, holy, holy, is the LORD of hosts: the whole earth *is* full of his glory" (Isa. 6:3). As a result of their adoration, "the house was filled with smoke" (v. 4). This smoke was the glory of the Shekinah Glory cloud that extended from heaven to earth and filled the holy of holies.

Isaiah repented, "Woe *is* me! for I am undone; because

I am a man of unclean lips, and I dwell in the midst of a people of unclean lips" (v. 5). He was overwhelmed because "mine eyes have seen the King, the LORD of hosts" (v. 5)—and God had said, "there shall no man see me, and live" (Exod. 33:20). Earlier, the phrase the LORD of hosts (*Jehovah Sabaoth*) was seen as a militant term describing Jehovah who led the heavenly armies into battle. The earthly parallel is of the king of Israel who led his armies against the enemies.

THE ROLE OF THE KING

Kingship had a twofold significance in Israel. First, the king was functional, i.e., he provided legislative, judicial and executive services for the people. Second, the king was symbolic, i.e., he was God's representative on earth. As such, the king took the place of God for the people. This is called ritual kingship or divine kingship. (When Jesus comes for the millennial Kingdom, He will fulfill both functions, inasmuch as He will rule the earth from Jerusalem, and also be the divine King who symbolizes the role of God in a theocracy.)

The functional king has several responsibilities. First, he has legislative power; he enacts laws. Earlier, on his deathbed, Jacob had predicted that Israel's king would come through the tribe of Judah. "The sceptre shall not depart from Judah, nor a lawgiver from between his feet, until Shiloh come" (Gen. 49:10). This prophecy has three aspects. First, it promises there would be a king of Israel. Second, the king would have legislative power to establish laws. And third, the king of Israel would come from the tribe of Judah. The psalmist reinforces this prediction: "Judah is my lawgiver" (Ps. 60:7).

The king's role as lawgiver would be similar to the

Congress of the United States (the House and the Senate), which establishes laws for the good of the people. Beyond the human king, God is the King/Lawmaker, "For the LORD *is* our judge, the LORD *is* our lawgiver, the LORD *is* our king; he will save us" (Isa. 33:22).

The second function of the king is to interpret the laws. This function is parallel to the judicial branch of the

---

Because God is our Father, the believer can presume upon His goodness. Because God is our King, the believer must submit to His sovereignty and control.

United States Government. On some occasions, the king served as judge, as did Solomon when two prostitutes both claimed the same baby. During the night one prostitute slept on her baby and it died. As king, Solomon interpreted the law. He decreed that the baby should be cut in half and each prostitute receive half of the dead body (see 1 Kings 3:16-28). Obviously the legitimate mother refused to allow the baby to be killed. "And all Israel heard of the judgment which the king had judged; and they feared the king: for they saw that the wisdom of God *was* in him, to do judgment" (v. 28).

A third function of the king was to provide services for the people such as roads and valid currency. This is the executive branch of government, or the aspect of the government of the United States represented by the president. In this capacity, the king would facilitate the civil functions of the government. The superior organizational ability of Solomon is seen in 1 Kings 4, where he established managers to oversee every aspect of his kingdom. This function was another reason why the people followed Solomon—"And God gave Solomon wisdom and understanding exceeding much, and largeness of heart" (v. 29).

OTHER KINGLY TERMS

Reign

The word "reign" is used interchangeably with king on many occasions in the Old Testament. It sometimes refers to the authority and power of the king, as in "The LORD reigneth" (Pss. 93:1; 97:1; 99:1). The fact that the LORD reigns is to be announced to the heathen (96:10). This may refer to the direct rulership of God that is similar to the theocracy of the judges. It also may refer to the fact that all kings actually reign only by the power delegated to them by the Lord, as in Proverbs 21:1: "The king's heart *is* in the hand of the LORD, *as* the rivers of water: he turneth it whithersoever he will."

Throne

The word "throne" is also used interchangeably with the words reign and king. The throne is the place where the king functions or sits as the divine representative. God does not sit upon a throne on the earth. "The LORD *is* in his holy temple, the LORD's throne *is* in heaven" (Ps. 11:4). God Himself enforced this truth: "Thus saith the LORD, The heaven *is* my throne, and the earth *is* my footstool" (Isa. 66:1). This reference to the localized presence of God is a figurative description, since God is omnipresent, meaning He is everywhere equally present at all times. The heaven where God reigns was thought of by the Jews as "the third heaven" (see 2 Cor. 12:2)—the first heaven being the atmosphere, and the second the stratosphere or the stars. God's throne was spoken of as being in the third heaven, from whence He rules the universe.

There seemed to be more than one throne in Israel. The psalmist notes, "For there are set thrones of judgment, the thrones of the house of David" (Ps. 122:5), apparently meaning that other bureaucrats or officials of the king sat on subordinate thrones or places of authority. These officials sat upon a lesser throne and functioned with delegated power from the king.

The psalmist also refers to a "throne of iniquity" in Psalm 94:20—probably a reference to a position of authority usurped by demons. The apostle Paul recognized thrones of spiritual authority—"whether they be thrones"—(Col. 1:16), suggesting angels who sit on lesser thrones than God, who are responsible for His work and who carry out God's delegated authority.

The throne was important because of its symbolic power. The Bible describes Solomon's throne in elaborate detail:

> Moreover the king made a great throne of ivory, and overlaid it with the best gold. The throne had six steps, and the top of the throne *was* round behind: and *there were* stays on either side on the place of the seat, and two lions stood beside the stays. And twelve lions stood there on the one side and on the other upon the six steps: there was not the like made in any kingdom (1 Kings 10:18-20).

The human throne had to be beautiful, impressive and

authoritative since it was the place where judgments were made and orders were given. More importantly, it was the place where the king sat as the divine representative of God.

The throne of God in heaven is described in even more awesome terms. John describes it in the book of Revelation:

> And, behold, a throne was set in heaven....And round about the throne were four and twenty seats: and upon the seats I saw four and twenty elders sitting, clothed in white raiment; and they had on their heads crowns of gold (4:2-4).

These elders apparently had delegated power from God. John saw angels ministering to God, a beautiful glass-like sea in front of the throne and the rainbow of God surrounding the throne. The beauty of the throne in heaven reflects the majesty of God who sits upon it. At this beautiful scene the angels can only say, "Thou art worthy, O Lord, to receive glory and honour, and power: for thou hast created all things, and for thy pleasure they are and were created" (v. 11).

APPLICATION

1. *Although God is as intimate as a father, as King He has sovereignty over our lives.* In the Lord's Prayer, Jesus taught us to pray, "Our Father which art in heaven..." (Matt. 6:9). God is a Father who receives us as intimately as if we were little children crawling into His lap. Hence, the believer can come into His presence anytime, anyplace and under any conditions. On the other hand, we must recognize the sovereignty of the King. As Queen Esther had to wait for

the extended scepter that gave her permission to approach the king, we must come reverently and carefully into God's throne room (see Esther 5:2).

After Jesus taught us to pray to God as Father, He then immediately told us also to pray "Thy kingdom come. Thy will be done" (Matt. 6:10)—tying the sovereignty of God to our intimate relationship with Him. Is it not interesting that we pray to our heavenly Father, but that He is referred to as having a *Kingdom*, not a family? Both the intimacy of fatherhood and the power, majesty and grandeur of a Kingdom are seen here. And at the end of the prayer, Jesus taught His disciples to pray, "For thine is the kingdom, and the power, and the glory, for ever" (v. 13).

Because God is our Father, the believer can presume upon His goodness. Because God is our King, the believer must submit to His sovereignty and control. In this analogy we see two sides of God, like two poles of a battery, brought together in the nature of God. Our heavenly Father is also the King of the universe.

When John F. Kennedy was president of the United States, he had the controlling power over one of the greatest nations in the world. Yet in many cabinet meetings, his young son, John, would run into the room, interrupting the cabinet members to climb up in the lap of his father. Should we do any less than young John did in presuming that he would be accepted by his father when we approach our heavenly Father?

2. *Jehovah Melek (The LORD Our King) deserves reverence and worship.* Often those who attend church forget to worship God. They learn from the Bible, they get caught up in the singing, or they are aware of their needs in prayer. But most believers are too concerned with their own desires, protection and self-will. Worshipers get wrapped in their own world and forget to center their thoughts on God.

We ask what we can get out of a worship service; it can also be asked of the typical church service: What did God get out of it?

Worship is not a nice addition for our church services; worship is a mandate. Jesus said, "the Father seeketh such to worship him" (John 4:23). As one person said, "Worship is when the worth-ship that is due to God is given to Him." Worship centers on God; worship is when the reverence and honor that is due to God are actually given to Him.

And how should we worship? Jesus reminded the woman at the well of Samaria, "God is a Spirit: and they that worship *him* must worship him in spirit and in truth" (v. 24). In saying that worship involves our spirit, Jesus indicated that worship involves all three aspects of man's personality: emotion, intellect and will. Worshiping in spirit involves pouring out adoration to God through such emotions as love, joy, praise and other deep feelings. Worshiping in truth involves worship based on the revelation of God. True worship must be based intellectually in cognitive knowledge of His Word. If we do not have a true understanding of God, or correct knowledge about Him, we cannot properly worship Him.

Much of modern worship is coined in a phrase using the word, "celebration." A worship leader may say, "Let us celebrate our salvation," or "Let us celebrate the holiness of God." As good as this is, it may make man the center of worship. A person may celebrate for the wrong reason, for what he can get out of it. Some make celebration like a Fourth of July picnic, or gift giving at Christmas—the significance of the event often lost in the way we celebrate it. Celebration may be man-centered; but worship is God-centered.

3. *A person enters the Kingdom by the new birth.* Jesus had

at least two major revelations in His teaching. First, the divine fatherhood of God, and second, the Kingdom of God and/or heaven. The doctrine of the fatherhood of God set forth that the individual could have intimate relationship with God. The doctrine of the Kingdom defines the collective and social responsibility of Christians as determined by the rule of the King.

Interestingly enough, the titles God the King and God the Father can be used interchangeably in many places. Jesus adapted the Old Testament idea of Jehovah as King to an inner and spiritual principle. He dealt with attitudes, motives and character. Those who live by the principles of the Kingdom of God live personal lives of godliness.

Jesus eliminated the exclusivism of the Jews in the Old Testament. Under His teaching, any person could enter the Kingdom of God. Still, there is a requirement: "Except a man be born again, he cannot see the kingdom of God" (John 3:3). To be born again, a person believes in the name of Jesus, which is receiving Him as Savior. Jesus went on to indicate that the virtues of the Kingdom were to hunger and thirst after righteousness, love, mercy, purity and peace (see Matt. 5:3-10). Therefore, the Kingdom has an inner dimension—there is love and grace to all who enter by faith. And it has an outward dimension—God as King governs the behavior of those who enter the Kingdom by the Word of God and by the leading of the Holy Spirit.

4. *The present Kingdom of God is different from the future kingdom of Israel.* There is a second Kingdom, the millennium (1,000-year reign), which is future in time. This is the time when Jesus will return physically and reign from Jerusalem. That Kingdom is in fulfillment of the promises of the Old Testament to the nation of Israel. That Kingdom shall be national and coercive. No one will live there by sin or selfishness. Jesus shall rule this Kingdom with a rod of

iron, and everyone will obey. This Kingdom is coming in the future when men shall see "the Son of man coming into his kingdom" (16:28).

The two Kingdoms, the inner Kingdom and the coming Kingdom, will be joined together in the future under the one King Jesus Christ. Jesus rejected the multitude when they came "by force, to make him a king" (John 6:15). Pilate humiliated Jesus Christ before a howling mob and proclaimed, "Behold your King!" (19:14). Pilate did not understand the future fulfillment of the Kingdom.

Under the present kingship of Jesus Christ, Paul honored Him, in writing to Timothy, as "the King eternal" (1 Tim. 1:17). As Paul ended the Epistle, he called Jesus "the King of Kings, and Lord of lords" (6:15). At His return, Jesus shall have "on his thigh a name written, King of kings, and Lord of lords" (Rev. 19:16).

5. *Today the King rules His subjects by yieldedness.* A person enters the Kingdom by doing the Father's will (Matt. 7:21). "For it is your Father's good pleasure to give you the kingdom" (Luke 12:32). Obedience is more than outward acquiescence; it is complete devotion to Jesus Christ and a serious attempt to please Him. This truth is described by Jesus, "But seek ye first the kingdom of God, and his righteousness; and all these things shall be added unto you" (Matt. 6:33).

We should pray for the Kingdom to come and manifest itself in our lives. Jesus taught His disciples to pray, "Our Father which art in heaven....Thy kingdom come" (Matt. 6:9,10). While this prayer related to the coming millennial Kingdom, it does not rule out the rule of God in our hearts at the present time. The prayer for the Kingdom to come is more than intercession. This prayer involves conforming our desires to His will, so much so that we are willing to conform our present life with the demands of the Kingdom. As we wait for His coming with anticipation, we conform our inner life to *Kingdom life,* hence preparing for the future Kingdom on earth.

CHAPTER 8

❖ THE LORD OF HOSTS ❖

The Militant Name of God

THE title *Jehovah Sabaoth* means The LORD of Hosts. This is another way of saying "God of the Angels."

The term "host" means army or other organized group; and the term "angels" means messengers. Thus, when God is described as "the LORD of the angels," it implies that He carries out His will by means of angels or messengers. Jehovah Sabaoth is the God of angelic hosts who carry out His will.

THE WORK OF THE LORD OF HOSTS

One task of angels is to transport people into the presence of God at death. To be "absent from the body" is to be "present with the Lord" (2 Cor. 5:8), and God uses angels to usher the dead into His presence (Luke 16:22). We should not fear death, because God is Jehovah Sabaoth, the God of the angels who accompany the dead to His bosom.

Another task of angels is to serve as guardians to protect us from physical harm: "For he shall give his angels charge over thee, to keep thee in all thy ways. They shall bear thee up in *their* hands, lest thou dash thy foot against a stone" (Ps. 91:11,12). (The indwelling Holy Spirit protects us from spiritual harm.) We can trust Jehovah Sabaoth because He sends guardian angels to protect us from harm.

The phrase "Jehovah Sabaoth" occurs 281 times in the Old Testament and denotes that the God of Israel brought heavenly powers to the aid of His needy people. As we shall see, the title first occurs in the book of Samuel when Israel was fighting for her political and spiritual life. Since the term "host" can mean heavenly host, as in angels or heavenly messengers, "the LORD of Hosts" could be interpreted as "the God of angels who fight for us." But the term can also refer to the armies of Israel (see 1 Sam. 17:45).

This compound name, the LORD (the self-existing and self-revealing One) and Sabaoth, or Hosts (multitudes in the service of God) told Israel that the God whose existence cannot be threatened by mere man was a militant God who would help them prevail against their enemies. David taught the people, "The LORD of hosts, he *is* the King of glory" (Ps. 24:10). As a heathen nation looked to its king to lead them into battle, God's people followed the LORD of Hosts.

THE USE OF "JEHOVAH SABAOTH"

The name the LORD of Hosts (Jehovah Sabaoth) is never found in the Pentateuch, Joshua or Judges. It rarely occurs in the books of Kings or Chronicles, and not much more than that in the book of Psalms. It is a phrase mostly related to the Prophets. The name is prominently used 80 times in Jeremiah, the prophet who wept over the destruction of Jerusalem. It also occurs 14 times in Haggai, 50 times in Zechariah, and 25 times in Malachi, the last book of the Old Testament. Why is the name so prominent at the end of the Old Testament? To answer this question, it is helpful to recall Israel's experience after the Exodus from Egypt.

When Israel was a fledgling nation coming out of Egypt, the people had a vision of capturing the land. Coming through 40 years in the wilderness, Israel rallied behind Jehovah and conquered the land of promise. Once the land was theirs, however, their lack of faith caused them to waver. At the point of wavering, the name Jehovah Sabaoth or the Lord of Hosts is first used to rally the people to battle and victory.

God's people had begun to capture the land in the book of Joshua, but they did not drive out all of their enemies. The next period proved to be disastrous, as the book of Judges shows. The people constantly returned to their sins, and to the worship of the gods of the Canaanites. When the name Jehovah Sabaoth was introduced, faithful Israelites were worshiping God at Shiloh, where the Tabernacle and Ark were located. Old Elkanah and his wife Hannah, the parents of Samuel, who would be the last judge, were among the faithful. "This man went up out of his city yearly to worship and to sacrifice unto the Lord of hosts in Shiloh" (1 Sam. 1:3).

The book of 1 Samuel is a transitional book, and Samuel is a transitional leader. Prior to Samuel, Israel was led by different judges who were military, political and spiritual leaders. When Israel followed the Lord, they were victorious. When they returned to their sin, God allowed them to be defeated. At their lowest level of depression and bondage, God raised up Samuel, the transition man, to lead Israel from a theocracy into an earthly kingdom, from leadership by judges to leadership by kings.

Israel grew dissatisfied with its judges and began to ask for a king like the nations around them—a strong military leader who could go before them in battle (see 1 Sam. 8:1-12). The problem was that their desire for an earthly king was really a rejection of God, their heavenly King. The Lord told Samuel, "They have not rejected thee, but they have rejected me, that I should not reign over them" (v. 7).

To Secure Victory or Judgment

The name LORD Sabaoth first appears to Israel as a nation in the context of this rejection of the God whose armies fleshly Israel could not see. In a battle with the Philistines, Israel was beaten, and approximately 4,000 men were killed. The leaders questioned, "Wherefore hath the LORD smitten us to day before the Philistines? Let us fetch the ark of the covenant of the LORD out of Shiloh unto us, that, when it cometh among us, it may save us out of the hand of our enemies" (4:3).

The people put more trust in a piece of furniture than in God. They knew that the LORD of Hosts was their militant Leader, because the Ark is described as "the ark of the covenant of the LORD of hosts [Jehovah Sabaoth], which dwelleth *between* the cherubims" (v. 4). They took the Ark into battle thinking they could not lose; but their faith was in a *thing* rather than in the LORD of Hosts. Israel was defeated and the Ark was captured.

Later, young David became the champion of Israel because he recognized the LORD of Hosts. When Goliath challenged Israel to battle, no one dared fight against him. Finally, David came to him with only a sling and five smooth stones. But David was not fighting with a man's strength, he was fighting "in the name of the LORD of hosts, the God of the armies of Israel, whom thou hast defied" (17:45).

Throughout the period of the kings, God raised up prophets to call the people back from their sinful ways and idolatrous worship. As Israel began to lose her faith, she lost her battles, too, because Jehovah Sabaoth did not fight for/with her. Perhaps the prophets used the name LORD of Hosts so frequently because they felt the defeat of Israel so keenly. Late in this period she was a captive people, and needed hope. Perhaps the name LORD of Hosts would reinforce optimism. Although the armies of Israel were defeated, God and His angels were not. Implied in the name is the promise of victory—if only Israel would repent, the LORD of Hosts would fight for her again.

Even though Israel had lost her battles, and the city of Jerusalem was destroyed, God still had His fighting angels. He remains Jehovah Sabaoth, the LORD of the angels. This name pointed the people to a new and higher spiritual

---

The LORD of Hosts has an army that obeys. There is no evidence of His having to punish the armies of heaven, because His angels carry out His will.

---

relationship to God as individuals, not just a return to the former corporate relationship that Jehovah had with the nation.

As we saw in chapter 7, Uzziah, a king who had been victorious for Israel, died during the days of Isaiah.

The young prophet of God had put all of his dreams into the reign of King Uzziah. After the king was dead, Isaiah saw a vision of the Lord and His angels. "And one cried unto another, and said, Holy, holy, holy, *is* the LORD of hosts [Jehovah Sabaoth]" (Isa.6:3). The angels who were part of God's hosts spoke the name Jehovah Sabaoth.

Isaiah was commissioned to go preach but was told

the people would reject his message. He was told Israel would be spiritually blinded and then punished. Hence, they learned that the LORD of Hosts (Jehovah Sabaoth) could lead into victory when He was followed, and He could punish when Israel rejected His leadership.

The punishment from the LORD of Hosts—on both Israel and her tormentors—is a recurring theme of the later prophets. "Therefore thus saith the Lord GOD of hosts, O my people that dwellest in Zion, be not afraid of the Assyrian: he shall smite thee with a rod, and shall lift up his staff against thee....And the LORD of hosts shall stir up a scourge for him" (Isa. 10:24,26).

After Israel was taken into captivity, God came to His people with words of both rebuke and encouragement. Earlier it was mentioned that Haggai constantly used the phrase, "the LORD of hosts." It appears nine times in the following passage emphasizing hope in what God would do:

> Yet now be strong, O Zerubbabel, saith the LORD; and be strong, O Joshua, son of Josedech, the high priest; and be strong, all ye people of the land saith the LORD, and work: for I am with you, saith the LORD of hosts....For thus saith the LORD of hosts:...Yet once, it is a little while....and I will fill this house with glory, saith the LORD of hosts. The silver is mine, and the gold is mine, saith the LORD of hosts. The glory of this latter house shall be greater than of the former, saith the LORD of hosts: and in this place will I give peace, saith the LORD of hosts...thus saith the LORD of hosts...In that day, saith the LORD of hosts, will I take thee, O Zerubbabel...for I have chosen thee, saith the LORD of hosts (Hag. 2:4-11,23).

To Secure Blessing or Judgment

At the very end of the Old Testament, the verse usually associated with storehouse tithing also linked the LORD of Hosts with either blessing or judgment:

> Bring ye all the tithes into the storehouse, that there may be meat in mine house, and prove me now herewith, saith the LORD of hosts [Jehovah Sabaoth], if I will not open you the windows of heaven, and pour you out a blessing, that *there shall* not *be room* enough *to receive it* (Mal. 3:10).

If Israel would obey and bring tithes to God, the LORD of Hosts promised:

> And I will rebuke the devourer for your sakes, and he shall not destroy the fruits of your ground; neither shall your vine cast her fruit before the time in the field, saith the LORD of hosts [Jehovah Sabaoth] (v. 11).

"Devourer" translates the Hebrew word for "eater," which is a reference to insects that, in time of plagues, completely ate all of the green vegetation. It is also another word for Satan (see 1 Pet. 5:8). The LORD of Hosts will protect both physically and spiritually those who tithe to Him.

Hence, we see two sides of Jehovah Sabaoth. First, He will attack the enemy as an offensive army and lead His people to victory. Second, Jehovah Sabaoth will guard or protect from enemy attacks, offering the faithful defensive protection from God Himself.

APPLICATION

1. *Jehovah Sabaoth brings heavenly power to the aid of His children.* This name, the LORD of Hosts, indicates the power with which God will help His children. When Israel came to the Promised Land, and their leader Joshua approached Jericho, he wondered how he could take such a city. On an observation trip, he saw a stranger standing before him. Joshua asked, *"Art* thou for us, or for our adversaries?" The reply came, "Nay; but as captain of the host of the LORD am I now come" (Josh. 5:13,14). Note that the Lord came to Joshua as Captain of the Hosts in his hour of need to encourage him. While not bearing the name Jehovah Sabaoth, it was the same Person who helped. Some commentators believe that this was a Christophany—that the One who appeared to Joshua in his time of need was Jesus Christ Himself.

2. *The LORD of Hosts rules the armies of heaven so they will obey His will.* The Lord has hosts who will not only fight for Him, they will obey His command. One of the difficulties in an army is getting the average soldier to obey. Sometimes threats of death, court martial or physical torture are used to get him to do so. But the LORD of Hosts has an army that obeys. There is no evidence of His having to punish the armies of heaven, because His angels carry out His will. "Are they not all ministering spirits, sent forth to minister for them who shall be heirs of salvation?" (Heb. 1:14).

How many are in the army of the LORD of Hosts? Jesus said on one occasion, "Thinkest thou that I cannot now pray to my Father, and he shall presently give me more than twelve legions of angels?" (Matt. 26:53). Beyond this number, the writer of Hebrews referred to "an innumerable company of angels" (12:22)—so many that they could not be numbered. The apostle John wrote in Revelation 5:11

that there were in excess of 2 million angels in heaven. This large group could not function efficiently without organization or a leader. The various groups of angels identified in Scripture all have their duty and their rank—and they obey their Leader.

3. *The Lord will allow His faithless people to be defeated.* There are two wrong ideas that Christians have about problems. First, some have the mistaken idea that being a Christian relieves them from problems and attacks. But a Christian will have pressures in life. "My brethren, count it all joy when you fall into various trials" (Jas. 1:2, *NKJV*). Note that James does not say *if* trials come, but *when.*

The second mistaken idea is that being a Christian automatically gives one the victory over all attacks. Old Testament Israel apparently had that idea. They felt that no enemy could defeat them because they had the presence of Jehovah in the Temple. They treated God like a rabbit's foot—as long as the Temple or the Ark was around, they could not be defeated. However, their sins of legalism, pride and selfish arrogance led to deeper sins of idolatry, adultery and even the sacrifice of their children in fiery holocaust.

The Lord of Hosts who would have defended Israel sat on the sidelines instead, and allowed heathen nations to destroy Jerusalem and the Temple, then rape the women, slaughter many of its population and take a large number of the people into exile (see 2 Kings 25; 2 Chron. 36:17; Zech. 14:2). God would have been honored by a victory against Israel's enemies, as a judgment of their enemies' sins. But the Lord of Hosts is also honored by the defeat of His people as judgment against their own sins. God does not enjoy the suffering of His people, but at times He allows it. Even then, His holiness is vindicated.

CHAPTER 9

❖ THE LORD/MASTER ❖

The Headship Name of God

WHEN a sales representative makes a presentation of his product, he calls his client by the proper title and name in order to help earn a contract. If he walked into a small hot dog stand and asked to talk with the executive vice president, he might be laughed at. Everyone would realize that the salesman doesn't know his customers. If he walked into the executive office suite and asked for an appointment with the foreman, he wouldn't get to see the president or the CEO.

Names and titles are important because they open doors. Wrong use of names reveals our ignorance, and says we don't know what we are doing or where we are going. Using wrong names and titles shuts doors because it shows we are not worthy of an opportunity.

We have seen that the Bible uses different names of God to reflect His different roles and functions. When we use the correct name in prayer, it shows we respect Him and know how to approach Him. I don't think God would refuse to hear your prayers because you used an inappropriate title. But your wrong use may reflect your spiritual immaturity, and the fact that you haven't taken time to get to know your Master well. Since His name is *Adonai* (Master), we who are His slaves should learn its meaning, and how to approach Him properly in that name.

Adonai comes from the Hebrew word *adon*, a word used to describe a master who owns slaves or a husband in his relationship to his wife (it does not imply that husbands own wives). Adonai is a plural form implying the Trinity. Just as *Elohim* is also plural, implying the Trinity, both are a reference in the Old Testament to the Father, Son and Holy Spirit.

The word Adonai (Lord, only the first letter capitalized) occurs 340 times in the Hebrew Old Testament. However, the rabbis eventually began to use the name Adonai as a substitute for the name *Jehovah*. Since Jehovah was holy, they could not even speak or write His personal name. On many occasions when copying the Scriptures, they substituted the word Adonai for Jehovah. Then to make sure that people knew that the terms were substituted, they prepared a parallel manual called the *Sopherim*, that listed the 140 times where Adonai was substituted for Jehovah.

Adonai expresses the personal relationship between a master and his slave. Hence it is a term that symbolizes the relationship of God with His people. The relationship does not emphasize ownership, but implies a working relationship.

Just as there is a relationship between a horse and his rider, there has to be a oneness between a person and God if they are to enjoy a "trust relationship." Hence, Adonai has a twofold meaning.

Master means relationship
Lordship means ownership

The relationship between master and servant does not begin with the servant but with the master, who must do two things for his slaves. First, he must provide for the needs of his slaves—a place to sleep, food, clothing and the basic necessities. Second, the master must give direction, training and accountability for the work of the slave.

Hence, the term Adonai puts more responsibility on God than on His people. In a sense the Master serves the slave, for once a person was a slave he looked to his master for direction, protection and care.

When Americans try to illustrate the master/slave relationship, it is tempting to think of the book *Uncle Tom's*

The name Adonai (Master) assures...the believer...that his God and Master has the resources and ability to take care of him. Hence, the Christian slave trusts his Master.

Cabin. But this would not accurately illustrate God's relationship to us because of the abuse of black slaves portrayed in the book. The relationship of slave and master in the Bible was more often one of love and allegiance. In the Jewish relationship, a slave had more privileges than the hired help. A slave could participate in the Temple sacrifices and was a member of the household. The hired help was excluded from these privileges.

THE MASTER/SLAVE RELATIONSHIP

The term Adonai (Master) explains the very heart of Christianity, which is the relationship between God and the believer. A Christian is different because he relates to

God; the world is the world because in practice it denies that relationship.

What does the name Adonai (Master) assure for the believer? First, it assures that his God and Master has the resources and ability to take care of him. Hence, the Christian slave trusts his Master for these things. Second, it implies that help is available to carry out the Christian's duty as a servant. Finally, a servant of the Lord has the privilege of calling upon his relationship with the Master to get the help that he needs.

The first time the word Adonai (Master) is used in Scripture reveals something about its meaning. Abraham had been in the Promised Land for 10 years. God had promised Abraham the land and a son—from these his great inheritance would come. But Abraham and Sarah were past the age to bear children. After 10 years it was only natural that Abraham was growing restless and impatient. He prayed, "Lord GOD [Adonai Jehovah], what wilt thou give me, seeing I go childless...?" (Gen. 15:2).

In this reference, Abraham has a burden for two things. First, he wants offspring—a son. Second, he wants the inheritance that was promised him. Perhaps Abraham realized that the inheritance was tied to the son. After 10 years Abraham did not have either a son or the Promised Land. Inasmuch as Abraham had a slave/master relationship to God, it was only natural that he came to Him using the name Master (Adonai) and Jehovah (the covenant-keeping God).

Again, Abraham prayed, "Lord GOD [Adonai Jehovah] whereby shall I know that I shall inherit it?" (Gen. 15:8). God had promised that He would take care of him. Now Abraham wanted some assurance.

Moses, the servant of God, also had a servant/master relationship with God. He felt inadequate when his Master commissioned him to go to Pharaoh and demand the release of God's people in bondage. Moses only had the rod of God against the power of the Egyptian nation. After offering several excuses to God, he finally prayed, "O my Lord [Adonai], I *am* not eloquent..." (Exod. 4:10). Moses had a speech impediment. Yet he knew he must speak to Pharaoh, king of the strongest nation on earth. So the servant went to his Master and asked for help. It was only natural that he used the title Adonai.

Joshua led Israel across the Jordan River and into battle against Jericho. Because God was with him, Joshua experienced a great victory (see Josh. 6). Shortly thereafter he allowed some of his men to go to battle against Ai. But there was sin in Israel's camp, and God's people were defeated. Joshua approached God in prayer (see 7:1-6). He went as a slave reminding his Master that he needed direction and power to conquer the Promised Land. Therefore, in this context it was only natural that Joshua used the title Adonai (Master). He prayed, "O Lord [Adonai], what shall I say, when Israel turneth their backs before their enemies?" (v. 8). The prayer of Joshua is based on his servant relationship with God. Obviously, God answered by pointing out the sin, giving them a strategy and finally a victory in battle (see 7:10—8:28).

Gideon was a young man who was fearful of the raiding Midianites who swept through the Promised Land destroying their cattle and their crops (see Judg. 6:1-6). The angel of the Lord came to Gideon when he was hiding in the valley in a winepress, threshing his grain. As background, only those who were fearful and hiding would have attempted to thresh grain in a valley. Usually the threshing floor was on the highest elevated peak, unobstructed so the wind could blow away the chaff. The angel of the Lord came to Gideon and said, "The LORD *is* with thee, thou mighty man of valour" (v. 12). This may have been an attempt to compliment or affirm Gideon, who was apparently an introvert with a self-acceptance problem. "And Gideon said unto him, Oh my Lord [Adonai], if the LORD be with us, why then is all this befallen us?" (v. 13). Gideon prayed to God in a servant/master relationship. He recognized that the Master could give him guidance and power. The angel of the Lord promised that Gideon was going to have a great victory, saying, "Go in this thy might, and thou shalt save Israel from the hand of the Midianites: have not I sent thee?" (v. 14). But Gideon still wanted answers from his Adonai Master. He prayed, "Oh my Lord [Adonai], wherewith shall I save Israel?" (v. 15). And based on this prayer, the Lord gave Gideon the direction for his victory.

Others in Scripture have claimed the relationship between slave and master in their service to God. When Manoah, who was childless, received word of God's promise of a son, he prayed to the Lord (Adonai, see 13:8). When Samson prayed to defeat the Philistines, he called upon his slave/master relationship (see 16:28). When David prayed to build a temple, he assumed a slave/master relationship. Since he knew that God would give his son, Solomon, His resources and His wisdom to build the Temple, David prayed as a slave, knowing that Adonai would supply (see 2 Sam. 7:18).

The psalmist joins the names Jehovah and Adonai in an outburst of praise in Psalm 8:1: "O LORD [Jehovah], our Lord [Adonai], how excellent *is* thy name in all the earth!"

When Isaiah was praying in the Temple, he saw the Lord (Adonai) high and exalted, sitting on the throne (Isa. 6:1). Isaiah's hero and friend, King Uzziah, had died of leprosy. Some might assume that Isaiah's personal world had collapsed. What he needed was a vision of his Master

Adonai. The Lord who was sitting on the throne was also Jehovah. For the angels about the throne said, "Holy, holy, holy, *is* the LORD [Jehovah] of hosts" (v. 3).

When Isaiah was called to serve the Lord, he was a proud, young diplomat/bureaucrat who worked for the king. He needed to be broken to enter into a master/slave relationship. Therefore, God showed Isaiah his sin and he cried, "Woe *is* me!" (v.5).

The call of Jeremiah had the opposite dynamic. Jeremiah was a weak man, apparently afraid of his own shadow. He is called "the weeping prophet." Jeremiah needed the same relationship with God that Isaiah did. He needed a Master, but he did not need to be broken; he needed to be encouraged. Jeremiah prayed, "Ah, Lord [Adonai] GOD! behold, I cannot speak: for I *am* a child" (Jer. 1:6).

God did three things to fulfill His role as Jeremiah's Lord or Master and to answer the reluctant prophet's prayer. First, He encouraged Jeremiah by assuring him that he would not have to rely on his own wisdom: "Whatsoever I command thee thou shalt speak" (v. 7). Second, God promised His personal presence in the midst of any critics: "Be not afraid of their faces: for I *am* with thee to deliver thee" (v. 8). And third, God gave his servant Jeremiah a vision of success: "I have made thee this day a defenced city, and an iron pillar, and brasen walls against the whole land...they shall not prevail against thee" (vv. 18,19).

APPLICATION

1. *As servants, our first duty is to submit to our Master.* The Old Testament Hebrew Adonai (Master) is the counterpart for the Greek New Testament *kurios* (Lord). Jesus Christ is the Christian's Lord and Master. He said, "Ye call me Master and Lord: and ye say well; for *so* I am" (John 13:13). He

also said, "The disciple is not above *his* master, nor the servant above his lord. It is enough for the disciple that he be as his master, and the servant as his lord" (Matt. 10:24,25).

The Christian should recognize Jesus as his Lord and submit to that relationship. Recognizing that relationship, the Christian who submits to his Master will hear the words, "Well done, *thou* good and faithful servant: thou hast been faithful over a few things...enter thou into the joy of thy lord" (25:21).

2. *We can trust the Master's care for His servants.* The title Adonai gives the believer the privilege of having Jesus Christ as his Master who will care for him, supply his need and give him direction in life. The Christian does not have to be anxious about his "daily bread"—supplying that is the Master's responsibility (6:11). The Christian does not have to fret over what job to do or where he should serve— there is a "Master" plan for his life (see Rom. 12:1,2). The Christian does not have to be concerned if he can do the things that God has for him to do—the Master promises the gifts of the Holy Spirit to enable him to serve God (see vv. 3-8).

CHAPTER 10

❧ GOD ❧

ELOHIM

The Strong Creator

RECENTLY a pastor came up to me at a conference where I was speaking. I barely remembered him as one of my students. He reminded me of all the things he did for me while he was in school. He claimed to have carried books for me and washed my car, plus some other things. I was embarrassed because I couldn't remember any of them.

As he left, the former student said, "Tell your wife Peggy hello."

I smiled, and suddenly felt better. I understood that the man had mistaken me for another professor, and that he really hadn't done for me all those things he claimed.

My wife's name is Ruth.

Names are important to people and their friends. When someone calls a friend by the wrong name, it probably means they are not as close as you are to a real friend.

When people say, "God saved me," or "I know God," although I do not question them outwardly I sometimes have my inner doubts. For God is an impersonal title for deity. All religions have a god. We who are saved use the personal name of the God who saved us. We say, "The LORD saved me," and we talk about "knowing the LORD."

The difference between God and the LORD may be very subtle to some, but those who know the LORD know the difference. The study of the word *Elohim* (God) in this chapter will form a basis for the study of the word *Jehovah* (LORD) in the next chapter.

God is a universal term for deity, used by almost all religions. To review, Elohim is one of the three primary terms used to describe God in the Bible. God (Elohim) is the strong Creator who is the source of everything. The LORD

(Jehovah) is the covenant-keeping God who relates to man. Adonai (Master) reflects the servant/master relationship of man to God.

Elohim comes from *El*, meaning "strong one" and *alah* meaning "to swear or bind with an oath." The term Elohim is used 2,500 times in the Bible to identify the Creator God, the One usually identified with this world, objects or the unsaved.

Elohim is the name first used for God in the Scriptures: "In the beginning God [Elohim] created the heaven[s] and the earth" (Gen. 1:1). The final reference to God in the Bible is the Greek word *theos*, in Revelation 22:19. The Bible therefore begins and ends with God, even though it includes many other names, titles or functions to give us other aspects of His nature and work.

WHO IS GOD?

There are many definitions of God. The God of the Bible is the Supreme Being, the divine One whom we worship. Definitions must have a definitive term, such as "the man is a husband." From the Bible we can draw at least seven definitive terms used to describe God.

Who Is God?

1. God is life.
2. God is a Person.
3. God is Spirit.
4. God is a Self-existent Being.
5. God is a unity.
6. God is unchangeable.
7. God is unlimited in space and time.

God Is Life

When Joshua told his people, "ye shall know that the living God *is* among you" (Josh. 3:10), he was giving one of the definitions for God. Even young David recognized this definition when he spoke of Goliath defying "the living God" (1 Sam. 17:26). To call God "life" is more than describing Him as the One who created life, or as the source of life. God is the essence or nature of life. The world may say that life is energy, power or force—or even "a bowl of cherries." But the Bible says that the life *behind* all these forms of life is the living God who used His energy to create the world. The energy that holds atoms and molecules together is the life of God. The Bible expands this truth when it says, "by him all things consist" (Col. 1:17).

God Is a Person

Whereas most of the religions in the world identify their deities by concepts such as a force or other kinds of impersonal beings, the Bible paints a higher picture of God. He has intellect, emotion and will, which are the elements of personality. In addition to this, God has self-awareness and self-determination. This personality of God is projected into man in what Scripture calls the image of God. Man mirrors his God when he exercises his personality.

The personality of God is seen in His intelligence. God knows (see Gen. 18:19; Exod. 3:7) and has infinite wisdom (see Jer. 51:15).

Next, God has feelings or emotions, sometimes called "sensibility." God feels grief (see Gen. 6:6), kindness (see Ps. 103:8-13), empathy (see Exod. 3:7,8), anger (see Ps. 7:11), plus a whole array of other feelings.

Then God has a will, which is the volitional reflection of His personhood. He can make decisions and choose His own actions. God is not bound by any force in the universe, for He is free. Because God has given persons an intellect in His own image, we can predict some of His actions. We know, for example, that He will always act in love. But we cannot coerce His actions, since He is perfectly free. No outside stimulus can make Him go against His will or choice.

God Is Spirit

In the New Testament, Jesus told the Samaritan woman, "God *is* a Spirit; and they that worship him must worship *him* in spirit and in truth" (John 4:24). Even though the *King James Version* uses the article "a" with spirit, God is not one spirit among many spirits. It means He is Spirit by nature. As such, God does not have a physical body; He is an incorporeal Being. God is a real Being who has personality and life, but does not live through a physical body.

Another way of saying this is that God is invisible. Some Bible references imply that persons saw God (see Gen. 32:30; Exod. 34:5-8; Num. 12:6-8; Deut. 34:10; Isa. 6:1). Actually, they did not see Him directly, but only a reflection of Him. The only ones who have seen God are those who saw Jesus Christ, "the image of the invisible God" (Col. 1:15). To say that God is Spirit is to say that people have not seen Him. One of the reasons the Second Commandment prohibits making idols or images is because God is not physical or material (see Exod. 20:4). He is Spirit, and He wants man to worship Him in His true nature.

God Is a Self-existent Being

Even though this chapter is defining Elohim, God's second name, LORD (Jehovah), indicates that He is self-existent. The name "Jehovah" comes from the verb "I am." When Moses prayed to God in the burning bush (see 3:1-15), he asked for

God to identify Himself. God answered by saying, "I AM THAT I AM" (see v. 14). This is another name for LORD or Jehovah. The phrase "I AM THAT I AM" actually means "the self-existent God." In essence, Jehovah is saying, "I exist by Myself and for Myself." The existence of God is not dependent upon this world, man or anything else.

God Is a Unity

The great *Shema* recited by observant Jews is based on the nature of God: "Hear (Heb. *shema*) O Israel: The LORD our God *is* one LORD" (Deut. 6:4). There can only be one God. To say that there are two supreme Gods or two Creators makes about as much sense as speaking of a square circle. There can only be one Supreme being; if there were two, these forces would clash. The nature of God excludes all others, for no other one can do what God can do. This truth is taught in Scripture: "Thus saith the LORD the King of Israel, and his redeemer the LORD of hosts; I *am* the first, and I *am* the last; and beside me *there is* no God" (Isa. 44:6).

God Is Unchangeable

Since God is perfect, He cannot become better; therefore He is immutable—He cannot change in His essence. And since He is perfect, He could not become corrupt and be less than God. The Bible states, "God *is* not a man, that he should lie; neither the son of man, that he should repent" (Num. 23:19).

This does not mean that God cannot change His mind. The *King James Version* says that man became so wicked before the Flood that "it repented the LORD that he had made man" (Gen. 6:6). God also "repented" that he had made Saul king (1 Sam. 15:11). But a careful study of such passages reveals that man turned from God in sinful rebellion. God did not change in His essence—consistent with

His unchanging nature, He judged man's sin. The real change was in man; and this called for a change in the way that God responded to him.

This is true even today. God is still unchanging, even though His way of responding to us depends on our response to Him. Obedience will bring reward, and disobedience will bring punishment. God does not change; man just moves from one side of God's nature to the other. The changing life-styles of man cause the consistent behavior of God to appear to change, but the essential change is not in God. He is unchangeable.

God Is Unlimited in Space and Time

In the beginning God created everything, including time and space. This means that He is Lord of time and space; He is not bound by His creation. The Bible says that God "inhabiteth eternity" (Isa. 57:15)—a realm beyond time and space. Abraham recognized God as "the everlasting God" (Gen. 21:33). Moses observed that "even from everlasting to everlasting, thou *art* God" (Ps. 90:2). The psalmist wrote, "But thou *art* the same, and thy years shall have no end" (102:27).

What is time? Time is the measurement of events that appear in sequence. God existed before the first event, Creation. He never had a beginning point, and will continue without a terminal point. He will always exist.

What is space? Space is all of the area where there is physical reality and being. Space is the distance between objects. But God is greater than space. "God that made the world and all things therein, seeing that He is Lord of heaven and earth, dwelleth not in temples made with hands" (Acts 17:24).

Since time and space are the results of God's creative acts, He is not limited by His creation. He is infinite in relationship to time (the sequence of events) and to space (the distance between objects). God is the only being who exists without limitations.

If there were another God, then Elohim would not be the self-existing, all-powerful, unlimited God. Since there cannot be two unlimited beings, there cannot be another God besides Elohim. For if there were another God, then neither God could be an unlimited God. The infinity and immensity of God are strong arguments for His sovereignty in the universe and in our lives.

GOD IS THREE-IN-ONE

If God is One, why is Elohim a plural word? Because the New Testament doctrine of the Trinity is latent in this Old Testament name, Elohim. God is a unity-in-plurality. Although the Trinity is not taught in so many words in the Old Testament, the footprints of the Trinity are found throughout its pages.

1. The compound unity implies the Trinity. The name Elohim is a compound unity. This is evidenced in several Scriptures. "Let us make man in our image" (Gen. 1:26); "The man is become as one of us" (3:22); "Let us go down" (11:7); "Who will go for us?" (Isa. 6:8). This does not mean there are two Gods, but that the One God manifests Himself in more than one personality.

Some modern-day Jews call this "plural majesty" instead of a Trinity. Queen Victoria is credited with the statement, "We are not amused." Although she was speaking only of herself, she used the plural "We," as is common among royalty. But the use of the plural in reference to God reflects more than plural majesty. It is God speaking to Himself within the three Persons of the Trinity.

2. Old Testament "blessing" formulas imply the Trinity.

The formulas for blessing in the Old Testament imply a Trinity. The Aaronic benediction was repeated three times: "The LORD bless thee and keep thee: the LORD make his face shine upon thee...the LORD lift up his countenance upon thee, and give thee peace" (Num. 6:24-26). The seraphim in Isaiah's vision of the Lord cry, "Holy, holy, holy" (Isa. 6:3), suggesting that each person in the

---

We must know God to know ourselves. Since we are created in God's image...the more we learn about God, the more we learn about ourselves.

Godhead is holy. Even the Hebrew *Shema*, which maintains the unity of God, implies a Trinity when it repeats God's name three times: "The LORD our *God* is one LORD" (Deut. 6:4).

3. *Three names imply three Persons.* Although some disagree, many Bible scholars believe that Isaiah 54:5 is one of the strongest references to the Trinity in the Old Testament: "For thy Maker is thine husband [Father], the LORD of hosts [Spirit] is his name; and thy Redeemer [Son] the Holy One of Israel."

4. *The Old Testament distinguishes between God and God.* Some Old Testament passages seem to make a distinction between God and God. Zechariah, speaking prophetically, writes: "And I [Father] will pour upon the house of

David...the spirit [Spirit] of grace and of supplications: and they shall look upon me whom they have pierced, and they shall mourn for him...*his* only *son* [Son]" (12:10). Psalm 2:7 says, "The LORD hath said unto me, Thou *art* my Son." And in Genesis 1:1,2, the Spirit who broods upon the face of the water is distinguished from God who creates the world.

5. *Clear statement of the Trinity.* Again, some scholars think that Isaiah 48:16 speaks clearly of God as a Trinity: "I have not spoken in secret from the beginning; from the time that it was, there *am* I: and now the Lord GOD [Father] and his Spirit [Holy Spirit] hath sent me [Son]."

So can we define God in one sentence? No! Even though the Bible has given us such information as that in the above description of God, a neat definition of Him escapes our finite minds. If we could define Him, we would be pouring God into the limitation of our words. God is ultimately greater than any of the definitions we give Him.

APPLICATION

1. *Cursing is prohibited.* The Ten Commandments prohibit a person from taking God's name in vain. When a person lightly uses the name of God, he is speaking lightly of God Himself. When a person curses by the use of God's name, he is rejecting God and His control in his life.

2. *We are to seek God by His name.* There is a clear command in the Bible to "Be still, and know that I *am* God [Elohim]" (Ps. 46:10). We are to seek and come to know God through His name, for it reveals to us the nature of His Person and His work. We should remember, however, that as we are searching to know God, He also is searching us and examining us. As David gave his son Solomon the plans for the Temple, he said:

Know thou the God of thy father, and serve him with a perfect heart and with a willing mind: for the LORD searcheth all hearts, and understandeth all the imagination of the thoughts: if thou seek him, he will be found of thee; but if thou forsake him, he will cut thee off forever (1 Chron. 28:9).

3. *We must know God to know ourselves.* "God createa man in his *own* image, in the image of God created he him; male and female created he them" (Gen. 1:27). Therefore, the more we learn about God, the more we learn about ourselves. Because we are created in God's image, we subconsciously long to become like our Creator. But a part of knowing ourselves is to realize that this longing can never be realized perfectly. The sin of Lucifer was thinking that he could become like the Most High (see Isa. 14:12-14).

4. *Knowing God leads to eternal life.* When Jesus prayed in the garden the night before His death, He said, "And this is life eternal, that they might know thee the only true God, and Jesus Christ, whom thou hast sent" (John 17:3). Those who know God receive eternal life. But it is impossible to know God without being saved. And the saved have learned of God by faith. "But without faith *it is* impossible to please *him*: for he that cometh to God must believe that he is, and *that* he is a rewarder of them that diligently seek him" (Heb. 11:6). And "If thou shalt confess with thy mouth the Lord Jesus, and shalt believe in thine heart that God hath raised him from the dead, thou shalt be saved" (Rom. 10:9).

CHAPTER 11

◆ LORD ◆

The Self-existent God

A little boy sat down at his kindergarten desk and announced, "I'm going to color a picture of God."

"But no one knows what God looks like," responded his teacher.

"They will when I get finished," the boy said, with child-like confidence.

Often we think we can determine what God is like by what we want, or by our need of the moment. But God reveals different names to us in our crises. The name *Jehovah* (LORD) is one of the earliest of His names that God revealed to His people to give them an indication of what He is like. Whereas the little boy's teacher was right—no one knows what the LORD looks like—we are given a word-picture of Him in this name.

The LORD (or Jehovah) is the second name used for deity in the Old Testament. The name God (*Elohim*), the universally recognized name for deity, appears first. But the second name, LORD, is the name that is used most often in Scripture, occurring 6,823 times in the Old Testament. And to modern Jews, it is the primary name for God.

Recall from chapter 1 that the word Jehovah or *Yahweh*—it can be pronounced either way—stands behind the word LORD, and that it comes from the Hebrew verb *hayah*, which signifies "to be" or "to become." (Remember, too, that it is spelled with capitals and small capitals in most translations, to distinguish it from Lord, [*Adonai*] Master.) When translated in the first person, it becomes "I am," said twice. Hence, when Moses anticipated that the Israelites would ask about God's name, God said to tell them, "I AM THAT I AM" (Exod. 3:14). Then the LORD said, "Thus shalt thou say unto the children of Israel, I AM hath sent me unto you" (v. 14).

The name LORD, therefore, points to the God who is continuously becoming—"the Self-existing One." He that is who He is, therefore, is the eternal One. Some interpret the name LORD as containing two truths in one name. The first meaning of LORD is "the One who exists in Himself," and the second is "the One who reveals Himself."

The name LORD goes beyond the meaning of the original name—God (Elohim) the strong Creator. God (Elohim) created the world in Genesis 1:1, but in Genesis 2:4, Elohim is identified as Jehovah (LORD God): "These *are* the generations of the heavens and of the earth when they were created, in the day that the LORD God made the earth and the heavens."

The second name, LORD, is perhaps God's favorite name. He told Moses, "I appeared unto Abraham, unto Isaac, and unto Jacob, by *the name of* God Almighty [*El Shaddai*], but by my name JEHOVAH was I not known to them" (Exod. 6:3). Throughout Scripture, God constantly refers to Himself by the name LORD, seldom by the name God. Why does He do this? Perhaps because there are so many gods, every false religion has its substitute god. But there is only one LORD who is the Self-existing One.

The uncertainty about how to pronounce the word Jehovah comes because there were no vowels in the original Hebrew. There were only the consonants that we transliterate into English as JHVH or YHWH. The vowels were developed later from pronunciation marks. Out of reverence for the name of the LORD, the rabbis in later Judaism would not write it or pronounce it—perhaps because of the verse, "holy and reverent is his name" (Ps. 111:9). Hence, the way they pronounced YHWH became obscure. (But they would write and pronounce the name God.)

The name LORD (Jehovah) is used in relationship to people, while the name God is used primarily in references that relate to nature or His creation. After Elohim created the world, the name LORD is added because the strong Creator wanted to relate to those He created. First, He is

> *The Lord [Jehovah] is the Self-existing One...and has many attributes of which we are not yet aware. Apparently He will continue to reveal Himself throughout all eternity.*

identified: "the LORD God had not caused it to rain upon the earth" (Gen. 2:5). Next we find, "the LORD God planted a garden eastward in Eden" (v. 8). Man was given the task of tending the garden. Finally, "the LORD God said, *It is not good that the man should be alone*" (v. 18). As a result of seeing the loneliness of man, "the LORD God caused a deep sleep to fall upon Adam" (v. 21). He took a rib from Adam, then "the rib which the LORD God had taken from man, made he a woman" (v. 22). Hence, the LORD God is concerned about man's relationship to woman, and about both man and woman's relationships to Him.

Next, the element of evil is introduced into the story because it broke the relationship between God and His created ones. "Now the serpent was more cunning than any beast of the field which the LORD God had made" (3:1, *NKJV*). Because they did not resist the serpent's temptation, Adam and Eve fell into sin. But a redemptive LORD came seeking them: "They heard the voice of the LORD God walking in the garden in the cool of the day" (v. 8). The LORD did not come to judge them, but ultimately to save them. He asked a question: "The LORD God said unto the woman, What *is* this *that* thou has done?" (v. 13).

The LORD warned the serpent that the seed of woman would bruise its head (v. 15). Here is the protoevangelium—the first hint of the gospel, the good news that Jesus Christ, born of woman, would conquer evil and be the means of salvation. But the LORD was not finished. "Unto Adam also and to his wife did the LORD God make coats of skins, and clothed them" (v. 21). In this act, the LORD obviously had to take the life of an animal, presumably a lamb. This animal became a foreshadow of all of the lambs that would be sacrificed for the sins of man until the ultimate Lamb, Jesus Christ, took away the sins of the world (see John 1:29). Hence, early in the book of Genesis, the name LORD reflects a redemptive relationship with man.

WHAT IS THE LORD LIKE?

In the last chapter, God (Elohim) was defined under the question, "Who is God?" In this chapter, Jehovah is described in answer to the question, What is the LORD like? The last chapter gave a definition of God, while here we focus on a description of the LORD.

God has traditionally been described by His attributes. An attribute reflects that which comes from the nature of God. As the rays from the sun give meaning to the sun and reflect its nature, so the LORD's attributes reflect His nature. People know what the sun is like because of its rays. In much the same way, we can know something of what the LORD is like from His attributes.

We will discuss six attributes in this chapter. The first three are called "absolute" or "moral" attributes because they deal with moral qualities that are beyond comparison with human attributes: The LORD is (1) holy, (2) love and (3) good. The second three are called "comparative" or "non-moral" attributes because they deal with natural attributes that to some extent can be compared with human qualities. Hence, the LORD is (1) omniscient or all-knowing, (2) omnipresent or present everywhere and (3) omnipotent or all-powerful. Some people believe that God has many other attributes that we will not know until we get to heaven. The hymn writer Charles Wesley spoke of God's attributes as "glorious all and numberless." Since the LORD is the Self-existing One who continuously reveals Himself, He has many attributes of which we are not yet aware. Apparently He will continue to reveal Himself throughout all eternity and we will continue to learn more about Him.

MORAL ATTRIBUTES

The LORD Is Holy

We have noted the description of the LORD as "holy, holy, holy" in Isaiah 6:3 and Revelation 4:8. Note that the word holy is repeated three times, perhaps recognizing each member of the Trinity, or each of the three primary names of God. The word holy means "to cut off" or "to separate." Hence, the person who is holy is cut off or separated from the world, yet separated to God.

It is important that we recognize the holiness of God because so much of our relationship with Him depends upon it. God is synonymous with holiness. "Holy and reverend *is* his name," said David (Ps. 111:9). Isaiah wrote about "the high and lofty One that inhabiteth eternity, whose name is Holy" (Isa. 57:15). Jesus called the Father "Holy Father" (John 17:11) and instructed His disciples to pray, "Hallowed be thy name" (Matt. 6:9).

Positive holiness. Holiness is both positive and negative. Positive holiness means the LORD is the personification of all that is good and pure. When John says, "God is light" (1 John 1:5), he is saying that God is pure, just as light is pure. The positive holiness of God means there is no sin in God's nature or in His presence. His people must be separated to Him and live holy lives.

Negative holiness. But there is a second aspect to God's holiness—negative holiness, which deals with the justice of God. Because the LORD is holy, sin cannot exist in His presence. When God must look on sinful people, He punishes sin. The judgment of the LORD is negative holiness. Hell was created because of this attribute of God: He must punish sin.

When we realize God is so holy that He must judge all sin, we begin to understand the necessity of coming to God through Jesus Christ. When Jesus hung on the cross and cried out, "My God, my God, why hast thou forsaken me?" (Matt. 27:46), we understand that God was actually unable to look upon His own Son as He died, bearing our sins. An understanding of the holiness of God reminds us of the degree to which God loves us. "For God so loved the world, that he gave his only begotten Son" (John 3:16).

The LORD Is Love

To understand God, you must understand love. Most people, in fact, describe God only with the attribute of love. But in God's case, love is more than an attribute, more than a virtue. Love is the nature of God. The Scriptures teach that "God is love" (1 John 4:8,16). When children are asked to describe God, they most often respond by saying, "God is love."

What is love? Love has been described as "a rational and volitional affection having its ground in truth and holiness"—an affection that "is exercised in free choice." Love is the attitude that seeks the highest good in the person who is loved. Love is basically an outgoing attribute, as expressed in an act whereby God gives to those outside Himself.

It is this outgoing aspect of God's nature that is highlighted by saying that God is love. Love is an attitude of giving one's self to another person. When God loves, He gives Himself to His creation. God created man because He wanted to share Himself with man. Because man is made in the image of God, man mirrors God. Someone described love as, "the perfection of divine nature, by which God is eternally moved to communicate Himself."

The apostle John describes love in these terms: "Greater love hath no man than this, that a man lay down his life for his friends" (John 15:13). Laying down one's life is the ultimate act of giving. Then John takes the definition of love a step further: "Hereby perceive we the love *of God*, because he laid down His life for us: and we ought to lay down *our* lives for the brethren" (1 John 3:16). Finally, John points straight to love: "Herein is love, not that we loved God, but he loved us, and sent his Son *to be* the propitiation for our sins" (4:10).

The love chapter of the Bible, 1 Corinthians 13, also describes love in terms of giving. The *King James Version* translates the Greek word for love here (*agape*) with the word "charity," which is now an out-of-date word. Charity today means giving time and money to a worthy cause.

But originally it meant giving of oneself to a needy cause or to needy people. Today that idea is conveyed by the word love. Since humanity is in profound need of the deity, it is a profound blessing that God can be described as the essence of love.

The LORD Is Good

When Jesus told the rich young ruler, *"There is none good but one, that is, God"* (Mark 10:18; see also Matt. 19:16-22), He was relating a truth the young man already knew. When God told Moses His name, He described Himself as: "The LORD, the LORD God, merciful and gracious, longsuffering, and abundant in goodness and truth, keeping mercy for thousands, forgiving iniquity and transgression and sin" (Exod. 34:6,7). Moses later told the nation, "The LORD thy God...will do thee good" (Deut. 30:5).

When children pray, "God is great, God is good, let us thank Him for the food," they are focusing on the most positive of all aspects of God, His goodness. The goodness of God is His mercy, kindness, long-suffering and grace that is manifested to those who are in misery and distress. The book of Hosea emphasizes this attribute. It pictures God's people as an unfaithful wife whom God pursues and wins back—not because of any merit of her own, but because of God's goodness and mercy.

COMPARATIVE ATTRIBUTES

The three remaining attributes discussed here are non-moral and comparative in nature, meaning that they primarily deal with God's power in relationship to Creation. The moral attributes deal primarily with His attributes in relationship to people. Each of the following attributes is introduced by the prefix "omni," which means *all*.

Therefore to say that God is omniscient means that He is all-knowing. Omnipresent means that He is in all places, or everywhere. And omnipotent means that He is all-powerful. These attributes of God show that human abilities reflect God's divine nature. Every person has a degree of power, but only God possesses omnipotence; everyone has presence, but only God is omnipresent; and everyone has some knowledge, but there is only One who is omniscient.

These three attributes of God may be defined by a comparison of the degree to which God and man share each characteristic. Psalm 139 lays a foundation for understanding the comparative attributes of God. The omniscience of God is seen in verses 1-6; the omnipresence of God is seen in verses 7-11; and the omnipotence of God is seen in verses 12-16.

The LORD Is Omniscient

The word omniscience has the word for knowledge or science added to the prefix that means "all." It means that God has perfect knowledge of all things at all times. He knows everything actual and potential—He "calleth those things which be not as though they were" (Rom. 4:17). The omniscient God has all knowledge in the world. God has never had to learn anything. He has never forgotten anything He ever knew. God knows everything possible. That means He knows and understands the sum total of all the world's knowledge and even those things mankind has yet to discover.

The Lord knows Himself, and He knows man. He knows His creation, because He is the Creator. David wrote, "Great *is* our Lord, and of great power: his understanding is infinite" (Ps. 147:5). Most Bible commentators agree that wisdom in Proverbs is personified in Christ. As Christians seek guidance in the daily affairs of life, it is good to realize that God guides us, because He knows the answers to questions we have not yet fully comprehended.

The LORD Is Omnipresent

This means that Jehovah is everywhere present at the same time. The psalmist asked the question, "Whither shall I go from thy spirit?" (Ps. 139:7). From heaven to the grave, early or late, near or far, God is present (see vv. 8-10). Hagar, Abraham's handmaiden, even named the LORD "The-God-Who-Sees" (Gen. 16:13, *NKJV*). The fact of God's omnipresence is a constant source of guidance, comfort and protection for the believer. We can never find ourselves beyond the presence of God.

Yet, God's omnipresence is one of the most difficult of His attributes to comprehend. The perfections of God demand that He exist everywhere at the same time. This does not mean that God is spread out so that part of Him exists here and another part of Him is in a room down the hall. Everything of God is here, in the room down the hall and in every other place at the same time.

The LORD Is Omnipotent

When we say God is omnipotent, we mean that He can do everything He wants to do. He can do anything that is in harmony with His nature. He can do the impossible (raise the dead; see John 11:1-44) and the improbable (walk on water; see 6:19). "With God all things are possible" (Matt. 19:26).

There are some things God cannot do, but they are either things that are contrary to His nature, or that are the result of His own self-limitation. Hence, they do not limit His omnipotence. God cannot deny Himself (see 2 Tim. 2:13), lie (see Heb. 6:18) or be tempted into sin (see Jas. 1:13). If God could do any of these things, He would not be God. This limitation represents things contrary to His nature. It is still proper to say God can do anything He wants to accomplish.

HOW TO KNOW GOD

The Bible commands that we know and love God for Himself. This creates a dilemma for mankind. Job experienced this dilemma when he cried out, "Oh that I knew where I might find Him! *that* I might come *even* to his seat!" (Job 23:3). Thus, the question is sometimes asked: How can a man know God?

By Faith
It is impossible to know God apart from faith. Faith is accepting what God says about Himself. The Bible says, "But without faith *it is* impossible to please *him*: for he that cometh to God must believe that he is, and *that* he is a rewarder of them that diligently seek him" (Heb. 11:6.)

By the Word of God
The Bible gives us a self-revelation of God. We see Him in the pages of Scripture. We can learn about Him through His names, actions, speech, miracles and manifestations.

By Desire
Some people are perfectly content to deny the existence of God without any serious consideration of the subject. These people are prevented from knowing God because they do not want to know Him. Unless people have a desire to know God, they never will. Why? The Bible says, "And ye shall seek me, and find *me*, when ye shall search for *me* with all your heart" (Jer. 29:13).

By Involvement

Our knowledge of God can grow just as our knowledge of a friend grows—but just as in the case of human friendship, this requires interaction and involvement with God. We must apply scriptural content to our lives. Jesus said:

> Not everyone that saith unto me, Lord, Lord, shall enter into the kingdom of heaven....Many will say to me in that day, Lord, Lord, have we not prophesied in thy name? and in thy name have cast out devils? and in thy name done many wonderful works? And then will I profess unto them, I never knew you: depart from me, ye that work iniquity (Matt. 7:21-23).

By Love

Knowing God is the highest privilege afforded to men. Unfortunately, most people fail to recognize the priority that ought to exist in this area. If the greatest commandment is to love God with our total being (see Matt. 23:37,38), then we must know Him to love Him.

CHAPTER 12

❖ THE FATHER ❖

The Intimate Name for God

THE favorite title for God used by Jesus Christ in the New Testament is Father (Grk. *pater*). In the Gospel of John, Jesus called God His Father 156 times. He not only claimed intimacy with the Father; He claimed to be one with the Father—which is one reason the Jews hated Him (see John 5:18). Neither the Jews nor their Scriptures regularly called God by the name Father. To them, God was the majestic, powerful Creator or Master. They did not know Him or approach Him in the intimate relationship as Father.

On a few occasions the Old Testament does identify God as having paternal instincts, as in Jeremiah 31:9 where God says "I am a father to Israel." But this was a metaphor or a picture, not a name or relationship. To Israel, God thundered from Mount Sinai in judgment. He was the Holy One in the midst of the Shekinah Glory cloud that rested in the holy of holies. The writer of Hebrews best summarized the Old Testament perspective of God: "For our God *is* a consuming fire" (12:29).

Jesus revealed a loving relationship with God by calling Him Father. He taught His disciples a new introduction to their prayers: "Our Father which art in heaven" (Matt. 6:9). Because Jesus' revelation of the Father was counter to the view of the religious rulers of His day, they wanted to stone Him (see John 5:18; 10:30,31).

To understand the Father, you must look to the Trinity. The Father, Son and Holy Spirit are all equal persons within the Godhead, yet one God. They are equal in nature, separate in person and submissive in duty. All the Father is in holiness, power and wisdom, so is the Son and the Holy Spirit. They are separate in person, for each has His own personality, i.e., intellect, emotion and will They are submissive in function, for the Father sends the Son and they both send the Holy Spirit (see 14:26; 15:26).

The first recorded words of the young Jesus revealed new truth about God. At age 12 Jesus said, "Wist ye not that I must be about my Father's business?" (Luke 2:49). Notice that Jesus used the name Father in reference to God, rather than to Joseph. We learn from this first reference

---

Believers...do not come to God in prayer as mere subjects to a king in his court. They crawl into the lap of a heavenly Father as a child who comes for protection or help.

---

that God is a Father, that the Father must have priority in our lives and that the Father sent the Son on a mission.

Because of the structure of the family, the world understood the nature and function of a father before Jesus revealed that God is our Father. This does not mean that the doctrine of God the Father gets its meaning from earthly fathers. Actually, the opposite is true—the human family on earth reflects the eternal family in heaven.

Since God is our Father, all who are saved enter a spiritual family. Believers have a spiritual kinship with each other and with God. Believers in Christ are brother and sister to one another. They are "sons of God" (see John 1:12) and "children of God" (see 13:33). As such they call God their

Father. They do not come to God in prayer as mere subjects to a king in his court. They crawl into the lap of a heavenly Father as a child who comes for protection or help.

Notice the terms used for God as Father in the New Testament: "O Father, Lord of heaven and earth" (Luke 10:21); "heavenly Father" (11:13); "the Father" (John 4:23); "my Father" (5:17); "God the Father" (6:27); "one Father *even* God" (8:41); "Holy Father" (17:11); "righteous Father" (17:25); "God our Father" (Rom. 1:7); "Abba, Father" (8:15); "Father of our Lord Jesus Christ" (15:6); "Father of mercies" (2 Cor. 1:3); "God and Father of all" (Eph. 4:6); "Father of spirits" (Heb. 12:9); and "Father of lights" (Jas. 1:17).

Some have interpreted the New Testament emphasis on God's new name, Father, to mean that everyone born in the world is a child of the Father in heaven. This view is called the "Fatherhood of God," which means that (1) all people are considered the children of God; (2) no one is considered lost; and (3) it is held that all will eventually go to live with the Father in heaven. This works out to the "Brotherhood of Man," implying universal salvation.

But the Fatherhood of God and the Brotherhood of Man are not biblical truths. Actually, the opposite is taught in Scripture. The Bible teaches that all are sinners (see Rom. 3:23); the wages of sin is eternal death (see Rom. 6:23); only those who believe in Jesus Christ will be saved (see Acts 4:12; John 14:6); and eternal life requires regeneration (see John 3:3,7).

WHAT DOES IT MEAN FOR GOD TO BE OUR FATHER?

After a Christian understands the nature and function of the heavenly Father he asks, What does it mean to me? The believer under the New Testament has certain benefits that were not available under the Old Covenant. In addition to a God who is majestic and lofty, the believer now has intimate access to His presence.

Fellowship with the Father
It is possible for us to crawl up in the lap of God as a small child will cuddle in the lap of his father for protection. "Our fellowship is with the Father," said John (1 John 1:3). God will protect His children even more than any father on earth will care for his child.

Access to the Father
No matter where we are, we can have immediate entrance into the throne of the majesty of God, who is also our Father. Paul notes that because we are adopted into the family, "We cry Abba, Father" (Rom. 8:15). He knows our needs before we cry, and we can go to Him at anytime.

Guidance by the Father
First, the Father teaches His children how they should go (see Ps. 32:8). Second, He actually guides them, through the indwelling Holy Spirit and principles of the Word (see Prov. 3:5,6; John 16:13). In the third place, the Father speaks through the conscience and will give guidance to His children (see Rom. 2:15).

Security from the Father
The Father wants all of His children, "to be conformed to the image of his Son" (8:29). Because of that He works all things together for good (see v. 28). But sometimes the Father must correct His children by allowing trials to come into their lives. Like most children, we do not enjoy laborious teaching sessions. However, the Father does everything for our good. "He that spared not His own Son, but

delivered him up for us all, how shall he not with him also freely give us all things?" (v. 32).

Inheritance of the Father

Because we are children of the heavenly Father, we are His heirs. "And if children, then heirs; heirs of God, and joint-heirs with Christ" (v. 17). All the riches of the Father will one day belong to those who are His children. Jesus promised, "In my Father's house are many mansions; if it were not so, I would have told you. I go to prepare a place for you" (John 14:2).

WHAT DOES THE FATHER DO?

The God of the Old Testament was Creator (*Elohim*), Master (*Adonai*), and the Self-existent One who gives life to His people (*Jehovah*). What could God as Father do for us that He could not or did not do before? When Jesus revealed God as the Father, a further self-revelation was given of God's nature and function.

A Father Gives Life to His Children

A child inherits his physical and immaterial nature from his parents. A child who is born again into God's family also gets several things. First, he gets a new nature, which is God's nature (see 2 Cor. 5:17). As such, he is known as a child of God. Second, he gets God's life, which is eternal life. He will live forever because he has the life of God in him (see John 3:36). Third, he gets a new standing in heaven. He is adopted into the family of God and is called a son of God (see Rom. 8:14-16). In the fourth place, he has new desires, indicating his new nature. He will desire to pray, read the Word and show forth the fruit of the Holy Spirit (see Gal. 5:22,23). Finally, he is now a member of the family of God. He calls God his Father, and other Christians are his brothers and sisters in Christ.

A Father Loves His Children

Many people think God doesn't love them when a calamity comes into their lives. This is a wrong view of God. God is a Father who loves His children, not a Father who hates them. As a result of this love, He will do good things for them. "If ye then, being evil, know how to give good gifts unto your children: how much more shall *your* heavenly Father" (Luke 11:13). Of course when His children err, there is a place for the heavenly Father to correct them, just like a father on earth. But the basic premise is that God loves His children.

A Father Protects His Children

The natural desire of every father is to protect his child. So the Father will give eternal life to those who trust in Him. "They shall never perish, neither shall any man pluck them out of my hand. My Father, which gave them me, is greater than all; and no man is able to pluck them out of my Father's hand" (John 10:28,29). The greatest protection of all is that no one can separate us from the love of God the Father.

A Father Provides for His Children

Many fathers work all week because they love to work. But underlying that, the truly loving father desires to provide for his wife and children. The Bible says, "And, ye fathers provoke not your children...but bring them up in the nurture and admonition of the Lord" (Eph. 6:4).

When an earthly father nurtures his child, he is providing him with positive training. Likewise, the heavenly Father will care for His children. "Wherefore, if God so clothe the grass of the field, which today is, and tomorrow is cast into the oven, *shall he* not much more *clothe* you, O ye of little faith?" (Matt. 6:30). The promise includes food, drink and other basic necessities, for as it concludes, "your heavenly Father knoweth that ye have need of all these things" (v. 32).

❧ A Comprehensive List of ❧ the Names of God in the Old Testament

The Primary Names of God

Elohim—God. The Strong Creator (Gen. 1:1).

Jehovah—LORD. The Self-existing One (Gen. 2:4).

Adonai—Lord/Master. The Headship Name (Gen. 15:2).

The Compound Names of the LORD God (Jehovah El and Jehovah Elohim)

Jehovah El Elohim—The LORD God of Gods (Josh. 22:22).

Jehovah Elohim—The LORD God (Gen. 2:4; 3:9-13, 21).

Jehovah Elohe Abothekem—The LORD God of Your Fathers (Josh. 18:3).

Jehovah El Elyon—The LORD, the Most High God (Gen. 14:22).

Jehovah El Emeth—LORD God of Truth (Ps. 31:5).

Jehovah El Gemuwal—The LORD God of Recompenses (Jer. 51:56).

Jehovah Elohim Tsebaoth—LORD God of Hosts (Ps. 59:5).

Jehovah Elohe Yeshuathi—LORD God of My Salvation
(Ps. 88:1).

Jehovah Elohe Yisrael—The LORD God of Israel
(Ps. 41:13).

The Compound Names of God
(El, Elohim and Elohe)

Elohim—God (Gen. 1:1).

Elohim Bashamayim—God in Heaven (Josh. 2:11).

El Bethel—God of the House of God (Gen. 35:7).

Elohe Chaseddi—The God of My Mercy (Ps. 59:10).

El Elohe Yisrael—God, the God of Israel (Gen. 33:20).

El Elyon—The Most High God (Gen. 14:18).

El Emunah—The Faithful God (Deut. 7:9).

El Gibbor—Mighty God (Isa. 9:6).

El Hakabodh—The God of Glory (Ps. 29:3).

El Hay—The Living God (Josh. 3:10).

El Hayyay—God of My Life (Ps. 42:8).

Elohim Kedoshim—Holy God (Josh. 24:19).

El Kanna—Jealous God (Exod. 20:5).

El Kanno—Jealous God (Josh. 24:19).

Elohe Mauzi—God of My Strength (Ps. 43:2).

Elohim Machase Lanu—God Our Refuge (Ps. 62:8).

Eli Malekhi—God My King (Ps. 68:24).

El Marom—God Most High (Mic. 6:6).

El Nekamoth—God that Avengeth (Ps. 18:47).

El Nose—God that Forgave (Ps. 99:8).

Elohenu Olam—Our Everlasting God (Ps. 48:14).

Elohim Ozer Li—God My Helper (Ps. 54:4).

El Rai—God Seest Me (Gen. 16:13).

El Sali—God, My Rock (Ps. 42:9).

El Shaddai—Almighty God (Gen. 17:1, 2).

Elohim Shophtim Ba-arets—God that Judgeth in the Earth (Ps. 58:11).

El Simchath Gili—God My Exceeding Joy (Ps. 43:4).

Elohim Tsebaoth—God of Hosts (Ps. 80:7).

Elohe Tishuathi—God of My Salvation (Ps. 18:46; 51:14).

Elohe Tsadeki—God of My Righteousness (Ps. 4:1).

Elohe Yakob—God of Israel (Ps. 20:1).

Elohe Yisrael—God of Israel (Ps. 59:5).

The Compound Names of Jehovah

Jehovah—The LORD (Exod. 6:2,3).

Adonai Jehovah—Lord GOD (Gen. 15:2).

Jehovah Adon Kol Ha-arets—The LORD, the Lord of All the Earth (Josh. 3:11).

Jehovah Bore—The LORD Creator (Isa. 40:28).

Jehovah Chereb—The LORD...the Sword (Deut. 33:29).

Jehovah Eli—The LORD My God (Ps. 18:2).

Jehovah Elyon—The LORD Most High (Gen. 14:18-20).

Jehovah Gibbor Milchamah—The LORD Mighty in Battle (Ps. 24:8).

Jehovah Maginnenu—The LORD Our Defense (Ps. 89:18).

Jehovah Goelekh—The LORD Thy Redeemer (Isa. 49:26; 60:16).

Jehovah Hashopet—The LORD the Judge (Judg. 11:27).

Jehovah Hoshiah—O LORD Save (Ps. 20:9).

Jehovah Immeka—The LORD Is with You (Judg. 6:12).

Jehovah Izuz Wegibbor—The LORD Strong and Mighty (Ps. 24:8).

Jehovah-jireh—The LORD Shall Provide (Gen. 22:14).

Jehovah Kabodhi—The LORD My Glory (Ps. 3:3).

Jehovah Kanna Shemo—The LORD Whose Name Is
Jealous (Exod. 34:14).

Jehovah Keren-yishi—The LORD the Horn of My
Salvation (Ps. 18:2).

Jehovah Machsi—The LORD My Refuge (Ps. 91:9).

Jehovah Magen—The LORD, the Shield (Deut. 33:29).

Jehovah Makkeh—The LORD that Smiteth (Ezek. 7:9).

Jehovah Mauzzam—The LORD Their Strength (Ps. 37:39).

Jehovah Mauzzi—The LORD My Fortress (Jer. 16:19).

Ha-melech Jehovah—The LORD the King (Ps. 98:6).

Jehovah Melech Olam—The LORD King Forever
(Ps. 10:16).

Jehovah Mephalti—The LORD My Deliverer (Ps. 18:2).

Jehovah Mekaddishkhem—The LORD that Sanctifies You
(Exod. 31:13).

Jehovah Metsudhathi—The LORD...My Fortress (Ps. 18:2).

Jehovah Mishgabbi—The LORD My High Tower (Ps. 18:2).

Jehovah Moshiekh—The LORD Your Savior (Isa. 49:26;
60:16).

Jehovah-nissi—The LORD My Banner (Exod. 17:15).

Jehovah Ori—The LORD My Light (Ps. 27:1).

Jehovah Uzzi—The LORD My Strength (Ps. 28:7).

Jehovah Rophe—The LORD [Our] Healer (Exod. 15:26).

Jehovah Roi—The LORD My Shepherd (Ps. 23:1).

Jehovah Sabaoth (Tsebaoth)—The LORD of Hosts
(1 Sam. 1:3).

Jehovah Sali—The LORD My Rock (Ps. 18:2).

Jehovah Shalom—The LORD [Our] Peace (Judg. 6:24).

Jehovah Shammah—The LORD Is There (Ezek. 48:35).

Jehovah Tsidkenu—The LORD Our Righteousness (Jer. 23:6).

Jehovah Tsuri—O LORD My Strength (Ps. 19:14).

❖ THE CAPITALIZATION OF ❖
THE NAMES OF GOD IN THE
KING JAMES VERSION

Old Testament Hebrew had no differences in type styles to allow for capitals, italics, etc. They were introduced by Sebastian Munster of Basel, Switzerland, in a Latin version published in 1534. The example was followed in several other translations, such as the *Geneva Bible* (1560), and the *Bishops Bible* (1568). The most extensive uses of special type styles appear in the *Authorized* or *King James Version* of 1611. There the translators used various combinations of capital letters to communicate the different meanings and interpretations of the names of God. Other English translations followed the practice. Those who recognize this use of capitals can gain insight into the nature of God and how He relates to His people, even without knowing the original language. Following is a guide to the use of these capitals in the *King James Version*:

God (first letter capitalized)—*Elohim* or related words such as *El* and *Elohe*, the standard term for deity in many world religions. In the Bible it refers to the "Strong Creator."

God (first letter capitalized, last two letters in small capitals)—This is the word *Jehovah* (Lord), as it appears with *Adonai* (Lord). Apparently the translators thought it would be awkward to translate *Adonai Jehovah* "Lord Lord," so they kept *Adonai* as Lord and translated *Jehovah* (JHVH or YHWH) as "GOD"—hence, "Lord God." When used in this combination, the term implies a headship relationship as that between a master and a slave, rather than emphasizing the self-existent and self-revealing aspects of the name Jehovah.

GOD (all three letters capitals)—This is the Hebrew word *El*, which is a derivative of *Elohim*. This title shows God in all His strength and power. It could be rendered GOD the Omnipotent (see Ps. 63:1).

Lord (first letter capitalized, last three letters in small capitals)—This is *Jehovah* (or *Yahweh*), the Self-existent and Self-revealing Deity. He is the One who was, who is and who is to come. Because He reveals Himself to man, He thus forms a relationship with His people. Hence, Jehovah is known as the Covenant-keeping Deity.

JAH (all letters capitalized)—The word *JAH* (or *YAH*) appears 49 times in the Hebrew text, but is translated JAH only once in the *King James Version* (68:4). *JAH* is a shortened form of the name Jehovah (or Yahweh), with emphasis on only one aspect of the name—salvation is to come. The full name, Jehovah, emphasizes past, present and future—"He who was, who is and who is to come." Most modern versions translate *JAH* Lord, since it is a derivative of Jehovah.

JEHOVAH (all letters capitalized)—God's name is printed in capitals in Psalm 83:18. Usually it is translated Lord. Perhaps it is emphasized here because it directly relates to what the name means: Whose name alone is JEHO-VAH.

Lord (only the first letter capitalized)—This is *Adonai* (Lord/Master), a term carrying the meaning of head-ship, such as a master who is over a slave. God is the Lord who rules over His servants.

God Almighty (first letter of both words capitalized)—This is *El Shaddai,* God who is the source of strength and comfort. The emphasis is not on God's creative power so much as His power to supply our needs.

Most High God (first letters capitalized)—This is *El Elyon,* God who possesses heaven and earth. This term is often used in relation to the Gentiles (see Deut. 32:8). It is used throughout the book of Daniel, which is set in a Gentile land. It is shortened to "most High" (first letter in "most" lower case, first letter in "High" capi-talized) in Daniel 4:17,24,25,32,34. It is printed lower case ("most high") in Daniel 3:26 and 5:18,21. In Genesis 14:8-22, where the name is first introduced in Scripture, only "God" is capitalized ("most high God").

The LORD Most High (each word beginning with a capi-tal, and the last three letters of LORD in small capi-tals)—Whereas the most common title is Most High God (*El Elyon*), a few references are to Jehovah Most High (see Ps. 7:17). Jehovah is used here because His covenant people are exhorted to praise Him.

Lord GOD (only the first letter of Lord is capitalized, and GOD is printed with capitals and small capitals)—This is *Adonai Jehovah* (or *Yahweh*). While Jehovah is ordi-narily printed "LORD," it would be awkward to translate the phrase "Lord, LORD" (see under GOD). "Abram said, Lord GOD (*Adonai Yahweh*), what wilt thou give me...?" (Gen. 15:2).

GOD the Lord (capital and small capitals for GOD, only

first letter capitalized in Lord)—Again, the name GOD is *Jehovah* (or *Yahweh*) in the original, followed by *Adonai*, but the translators wanted to avoid the repetition of "LORD the Lord." Here, however, the context seems to call for repetition for emphasis: "God the God (*El...El*)...LORD the Lord (*Yahweh Adonai*).

Random Capitalization

The following phrases were capitalized to show the importance the *King James* translators gave to the name of God. Many modern scholars find no basis for printing the titles in capitals, except to show respect for the names and qualities of the Deity.

I AM THAT I AM (Exod. 3:14).

I AM (Exod. 3:14).

JEHOVAH (Exod. 6:3; Ps. 83:18; Isa. 26:4).

HOLINESS TO THE LORD (Exod. 28:36).

THE LORD THY GOD (Deut. 28:58).

THE LORD OUR RIGHTEOUSNESS (Jer. 23:6).

BRANCH (Zech. 3:8; 6:12).